...erife
Canary Islands

2nd Edition

Original publication 2003
Reprinted 2012
Second reprint 2018

Robin Gill and Matthew Thirlwall

Edited by

J. T. Greensmith

CONTENTS   page

LIST OF FIGURES

INTRODUCTION

Tenerife, the largest of the Canary Islands, is dominated by the impressive 3,718 m (12,195 ft) stratovolcanic cone of Teide, the highest peak in Spain. As well as offering dramatic scenery in a pleasant climate, the island provides outstanding examples of a wide range of volcanic processes. Moreover, a lot of new research has been published on Tenerife since the first edition of this Guide came out in 1994, offering new insights into, for example, the cyclicity of ignimbrite eruption and caldera subsidence, the processes by which welded pyroclastic deposits may be emplaced, and the huge scale of landslides that have contributed to the present landscape of the island. These new results make Tenerife a still more attractive and fascinating tour venue for the amateur volcanologist and an outstanding teaching resource for university Earth science departments. This new enlarged GA Guide aims to acquaint volcanophiles with the current state of understanding, applied to a wider range of key localities.

The age of the island is not well established, but current literature suggests that the oldest exposed lavas are 11-12 million years (Ma) old, slightly younger than the Miocene shield basalts of Gran Canaria (~13.5 Ma). There is much exceptionally well exposed volcanic geology to be seen on Tenerife (Figure 1). This includes a wide range of basaltic volcanic features (**pahoehoe**[1] and **a'a** basalt flows, exposed **lava tubes**, dissected **scoria cones**, *etc.*), outstanding **felsic** pyroclastic sequences (**plinian pumice** fall deposits, thick **unwelded ignimbrites**, **welded** and **rheomorphic fire fountain** deposits, **pyroclastic surge** deposits, various forms of felsic lava dome (**exogenous, endogenous**) as well as active fumaroles. The field geology of the topographically preserved Cañadas **caldera** and the superimposed Teide and Pico Viejo cones (Figure 25) is superb. Above all there is the excitement of a whiff of sulphur on an active volcano that last erupted in 1909 and will undoubtedly do so again before long.

Many of the volcanic features listed above are characteristic of silicic calc-alkaline volcanoes (dacite and rhyolite) associated with convergent plate margins, but in Tenerife they are the product instead of **silica-undersaturated** alkaline volcanism (**trachyte** and **phonolite**) in an intra-plate setting. One must therefore avoid adjectives such as 'acid' and 'silicic' that instinctively spring to mind for highly **evolved** magmas, and refer instead to '**felsic**' compositions, a term that can

---

[1] *Terms printed in bold are explained in the Glossary at the end of this Guide.*

Introduction

be applied to oversaturated *and* undersaturated residual melts.

This Guide is written both for the amateur enthusiast and for professional colleagues. We hope the former will find the Glossary of current volcanological usage in Appendix I and the explanatory boxes in the text useful; further back-ground reading can be found in standard textbooks such as Thorpe and Brown (1991), Fisher and Schmincke (1985), Cas and Wright (1987), Francis (1993), Fisher *et al.* (1997) and Rothery (2001). There are also numerous websites devoted to volcano topics, where further information and pictures can be sought. Among the best are:

https://volcano.si.edu/
    The *Global Volcanism Program* site run by the Smithsonian Institution

http://volcano.oregonstate.edu
    Volcano World, a very useful site at the Oregon State University

http://bit.ly/2on3j7h
    A helpful illustrated glossary of volcanic terms

For the professional geologist we have provided a list of literature references, which is, however, not exhaustive.

LOGISTICS

Package holidays to Tenerife usually include charter flight, accommodation in self-catering apartments or hotels, and coach transport between airport and accommodation. They are available from many tour operators. Package tours including resort accommodation are generally the cheapest option, especially for parties of more than a few people.

Holiday centres providing resort accommodation are mostly located (a) in the south of the island, around Playa de las Americas, Los Cristianos, Las Galletas and Los Gigantes and (b) in the north around Puerto de la Cruz, which offers a little more local colour. The resorts in the south offer good access to the Bandas del Sur and the Roque del Conde and Teno massifs. The north and northeast of the island are more remote and are more accessible from Puerto de la Cruz or La Laguna. For those not tied to package tour resorts, Vilaflor makes an excellent centre, as does the Parador de Las Cañadas del Teide in the caldera (http://bit.ly/2sKhd88) for those who can afford it. UK travel agents and carriers can arrange hire vehicles in advance: cars seating 4-5 people are available at standard rates; 9-seater minibuses can also be rented. Most of the outcrops described in this guide have safe parking for 3-4 cars nearby. The small print of rental contracts may exclude driving on unmetalled roads.

The Tenerife climate allows field excursions throughout the year, with daytime temperatures ranging from 15 to 25°C between winter and summer at the coast, and some 10° less in the Las Cañadas caldera at around 2000m above sea level. Winter visitors may encounter snow in Las Cañadas, and should go prepared for bitterly cold temperatures there and on Teide, especially early in the morning. The cable-car up Teide does not operate on icy or windy days. Precipitation varies substantially across the island: the south is generally drier throughout the year, though week-long periods of winter rain have become more common in recent years; the northeast tends to have wetter weather throughout the year. Cloud and mist may build up around the flanks of Las Cañadas, but the caldera area itself often remains above the cloud.

The costs of package holidays from the UK are lowest in November and December (excluding the Christmas period), but one can obtain inexpensive late deals at any time of year, except for school holidays.

The topographically most accurate maps available are the 1:25,000 military series but each sheet covers only a small area of the island. The best general touring map available is the double-sided 1:50,000 *Kompass* walking and road-touring map No 233, price about £10 + p&p[2]. As well as showing walking trails and correctly numbered and signed motorway exits, it features town plans of most urban centres, though no tourist map can be relied on to guide you through the maze of minor streets that characterize most Tenerife towns or villages. The *Rough Guide* to Tenerife and La Gomera (published in 2001 at £5.99[3]) provides a lot of general tourist information and lists places to stay away from the main resorts. Visitors wishing to combine geology with a walking holiday in Tenerife will find the Cicerone guide *Walking on Tenerife* useful (https://bit.ly/2IMoWH5).

Visiting other Canary islands from Tenerife is not as easy as one might expect. La Gomera is about 60 minutes by hydrofoil from Los Cristianos and provides a possible day trip, but in general Tenerife car hire companies do not allow their vehicles to be taken off the island and therefore a separate rental would be needed on La Gomera. The other islands may be reached only by longer sea journeys or by air.

---

[2] *Giving precise directions in this Guide has been complicated by the re-numbering of all Tenerife roads, not shown on the current Kompass map at the time of writing (corrected edition due in 2004). A convenient up-to-date road map available at the time of writing is the 1:100k Indestructible Map of Tenerife (£4.99 ISBN 1904418007 available from amazon.co.uk) . The new road numbers have been adopted in this Guide.*

[3] *https://bit.ly/2IOxVHx*

Logistics

Personal Safety

A geological visit to Tenerife at any season requires careful preparation. The latitude of the island means that sea-level temperatures can be balmy throughout the year, but more severe conditions may be encountered in the caldera or near the summit of Teide, especially in winter, owing to their high altitude. Visitors should be equipped with water, sunscreen and a sunhat at all times of year. Winter visitors to the caldera and Teide should be prepared for bitingly cold winds, heavy frost, icy roads and trails, and significant snow cover (which may block roads and paths), and should therefore equip themselves as they would for the Lake District in winter: hat, gloves, warm and windproof clothing, rainwear, first-aid kit, torch (evening light fades rapidly at these latitudes), bivouac bag and reserve food. Snow rapidly becomes icy so must be treated with great caution.

All of the roadside stops listed here require careful attention to passing traffic, as local roads are both winding - with many blind bends - and heavily used; a light-weight high-visibility vest is strongly recommended, and party leaders should designate a responsible person to slow down approaching traffic and to clear the party from the road whenever traffic does approach.

The off-road excursions listed in this Guide vary considerably in the demands they make on the visitor and the potential hazards they present (see gradings page 19). None of them requires activities that a fit, experienced hill-walker would consider reckless but all require careful attention to personal safety, and the visitor is urged (especially if leading a group) to make a conscious mental assessment of potential hazards at each stop before becoming absorbed in the geology and to adopt the normal precautions. Three hazards command particular attention in Tenerife.

- *remoteness:* some walks (e.g.7.1, 8.3) cross infrequently visited wilderness country, and no visitor should attempt off-road excursions alone. Ensure a contact knows your intended route and carry a mobile phone at all times.
- *rough terrain:* lava fields are unforgiving to fall on, especially the glassy obsidian flows of Teide, and a pair of trekking poles may prove helpful. If your balance and agility are not good, do not attempt such routes.
- *altitude:* the caldera floor varies between 1950m and 2350m above sea level and the summit of Teide is over 3700m. For those prone to altitude sickness, heart conditions or high blood pressure, the danger of driving from sea-level and immediately taking the cable car up Teide should not be under-estimated; consult your doctor and insurer *before* making the trip. It may be prudent to spend a night or two acclimatizing in Vilaflor or at the Parador.

THE CANARY ISLANDS

The Canary Islands constitute one of the world's major oceanic volcanic-island groups. They stand on the northwest African continental rise and slope, and extend westwards for about 500 km from the easternmost island, Lanzarote, which is 150 km from the African coast. The islands lie 2000 km from the Mid-Atlantic Ridge on oceanic crust older than 150 Ma. The volcanic history of the Canaries goes back more than 20 Ma; however all of the islands except one (La Gomera) have been volcanically active in historic or recent pre-historic times. The recent discovery by sonar sidescan of young seamounts SW of Hierro (Rihn *et al.* 1998) suggests that the construction of new volcanic islands is continuing.

Only about 5% of the volume of each island is exposed subaerially. Rocks probably similar to Tenerife's submarine 'basement' are exposed in Fuerteventura and La Palma, where they include a central plutonic complex (mostly gabbro), a sheeted dyke complex, pillow lavas, pillow breccias and hyaloclastites; on Fuertaventura the pillow-lava sequence is ~650m thick and is succeeded by a 1150m-thick upper extrusive sequence composed of pillow breccias and hyaloclastites.

Intra-plate oceanic islands like Tenerife and Gran Canaria generally show at least two phases of subaerial activity: a *shield-building phase* (the 'Old Basaltic Series' of Tenerife) that constructed one or more basaltic shield volcanoes (sometimes with more evolved products too, like the voluminous rhyolites of Gran Canaria), and a smaller-volume *post-erosional phase* that followed a hiatus in volcanic output in which significant erosion of the volcanic edifice took place. Tenerife is a typical intra-plate oceanic island, except that its post-erosional phase exhibits an unusually high proportion of evolved **trachytic** and silica-undersaturated **phonolitic** volcanic products.

The origin of Canary Island magmatism has been focus of controversy for many years and is still not fully understood. The islands are much younger (22 Ma to the present) than the ocean crust on which they stand (155 Ma). They happen to lie close to the SW extension of the South Atlas Fault Zone, and Anguita and Hernán (1975) attributed Canaries volcanism to NNW-SSE extension of the oceanic lithosphere as it accommodated compressional deformation in the Atlas-Rif-Betic orogen to the northeast. Most authors today, however, interpret the islands as the product of some form of hot spot or mantle plume. Like the Hawaiian islands, the Canaries form an array of islands, elongated in the direction of plate motion, whose initiation ages (based on dating of the oldest subaerial lavas on each island) correlate with position in the chain. Any parallel drawn between the Canaries and the

The Canary Islands

Hawaiian islands must however take account of a number of marked differences.

- The age trend, like the geographical distribution (Figure 1 inset), is far less regular than for the Hawaiian chain (see Carracedo *et al* 1998, fig. 2). Moreover volcanism has taken place on all islands (except La Gomera) in the last 5 ka, implying a dispersed melting anomaly beneath the entire island group.
- No large-amplitude sea-floor topographic swell is associated with the Canary Islands, suggesting a less powerful heat source than exists beneath Hawaii or plume-related Atlantic archipelagos such as the Cape Verde islands.
- Individual Canary islands remain active, with one or more hiatuses, for much longer than Hawaiian islands and seamounts; this may in part reflect the African plate's lower plate velocity compared to the Pacific.
- Melt productivity rates ($km^3 Ma^{-1}$) are lower for the Canaries than for the

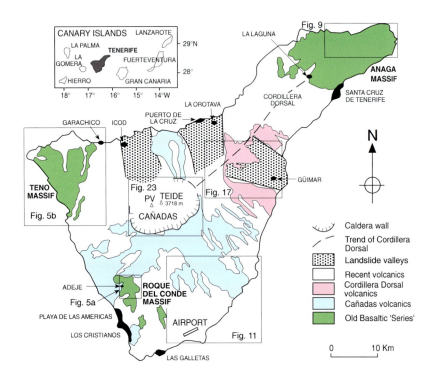

Figure 1. A simplified geological map of Tenerife (based on Ancochea et al. 1990 and Huertas et al. 2002) showing the areas covered by more detailed locality maps.

Hawaiian islands, and there is no petrological evidence (e.g. MgO-rich picrites as seen in Hawaii or Iceland) for elevated degrees of melting associated with a high-temperature plume.

The complexity of volcanic evolution for individual islands, the differences between island histories, and the geochemical variability of the sources feeding them are hard to reconcile with the operation of a vigorous steady-state plume. Hoernle and Schmincke (1993) proposed a 'blob' model, in which a feebly upwelling mantle plume breaks up during ascent into blobs of deep-mantle material separated by entrained asthenosphere, to explain the variability of magma geochemistry in space and time: each island may be the product of several blobs of subtly different geochemistry, undergoing decompression melting one after the other to generate a succession of volcanic cycles.

VOLCANIC EVOLUTION OF TENERIFE

Figure 1 shows a simplified geological map of Tenerife; Figure 2 illustrates the evolution of Tenerife in cartoon form, and Table 1 outlines the stratigraphic and geochronological framework. The reader may consult Ancochea *et al.* (1990, 1999),

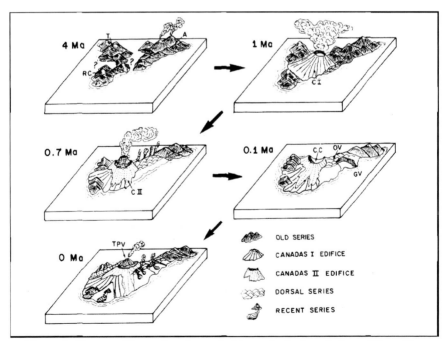

Figure 2. Cartoon illustrating the probable geological evolution of Tenerife (reproduced with permission of Elsevier from Ancochea et al. 1990).

Table 1: Volcanic stratigraphy of Tenerife

Main units	Stratigraphy	Type of product	Distribution	Age range	Collapses
Post-erosional phase					
Historic eruptions		Primitive and evolved basanites	Cordillera Dorsal, Puerto de la Cruz area, and Santiago area	1430-1909 AD	
Pico Viejo-Teide edifice	See Ablay et al (1998)	Basanite to phonolite lineages	Las Cañadas caldera floor and northern flank	168 ka to Recent	
Cordillera Dorsal volcanism	(only minor unconformities)	Alkali basalt and ankaramite flows and scoria cones	Cordillera Dorsal	0.90 - 0.43 Ma[1]	Orotava[4] / Güímar[3] / Caldera formation 1.5 - 0.17 Ma
Cañadas stratovolcano	Upper Group	Cycles of alkali basalt, trachy-basalt and phonolite, including large ignimbrite eruptions associated with multicyclic caldera formation	The 'Bandas del Sur' to the S, SE and E of the present Las Cañadas caldera. Also exposed in the NE, S, SE and E sectors of the caldera wall. See Table 2	1.5 - 0.168 Ma[2]	
	Lower Group[6]	Basalt, trachybasalt, trachyte and phonolite lavas and ignimbrites	Base of caldera wall (+ Tigaiga massif, Adeje, Las Americas[6])	3.3 - 2.0 Ma[5]	
	E r o s i o n a l u n c o n f o r m i t y				
Shield-building phase					
Old Basalt 'Series' (OBS)		Alkali basalt, ankaramite and basanite lava flows and scoria cones and varying proportions of trachyte; volcaniclastic layers and sub-volcanic intrusions	• Anaga massif (NE) • Teno massif (W) • Roque del Conde massif (S)	8.0 - 4.2 Ma[7] 6.4 - 6.0 Ma[7] ~ 11 Ma[7]	

Overlap / Flank basalts

[1] Ancochea et al (1990)
[2] Brown et al (2003)
[3] Constrained between 0.83 and 0.29 Ma (Brown et al, 2003).
[4] Constrained between 0.87 and 0.56 Ma (Ancochea et al, 1990).
[5] Martí et al (1994) based on the oldest outcrops in the caldera wall.
[6] Ancochea et al (1999) and Huertas et al (2002) challenge this sub-division. On the basis of Ar-Ar ages from Cañadas outcrops on the flanks of the island, they divide the stratigraphy into Cañadas I (3.5-3.0 Ma), Cañadas II (2.5-1.4 Ma) and Cañadas III (1.4-0.17 Ma) cycles.
[7] Thirlwall et al (2000)

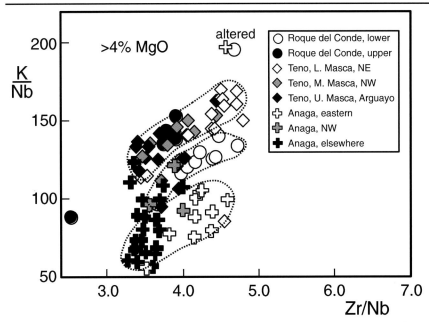

Figure 3. K/Nb ratios versus Zr/Nb ratios in Tenerife older basalts, adapted from Thirlwall et al. (2000, fig. 13). K, Nb, and Zr are incompatible trace elements. Nb/Zr ratios are affected by differences in partial melting history, but these effects are minimised by plotting only basaltic compositions (MgO>4%). The differences in K/Nb point to differences in source composition between the three massifs.

Araña & Coello (1989) and Martí & Mitjavila (1995) for details. The term 'Series' is commonly used in the Spanish literature on Tenerife; in this Guide we place the term in quotes to emphasise that it does not comply with modern lithostratigraphic usage.

The Basalts of the Shield-Forming Phase

The Old Basaltic 'Series' ('OBS') of Fuster *et al.* (1968) consists of late-Miocene to Pliocene basalt, **ankaramite** and **basanite** lavas and pyroclastic rocks, with a generally small proportion of felsic differentiates (commonly as late dykes and domes). The OBS is preserved with thicknesses exceeding 1km in three geographically separate rugged massifs, which originally may have formed distinct islands (Figures 1 and 2): the Roque del Conde massif in the Adeje area in the south of the island, the Teno massif in the northwest, and the Anaga massif in the northeast. **Argon-argon ages** for the subaerial parts of these successions range from 11.3 Ma to about 4.2 Ma (Thirlwall *et al.* 2000; see Table 1). The fairly distinct trace element (Figure3) and isotopic signatures of the three massifs point to significant differences between

The volcanic evolution of Tenerife

the mantle source regions supplying melts to each massif, and this evidence, combined with their different age ranges (Table 1), supports the suggestion by Ancochea *et al.* (1990) that the massifs may initially have developed as three separate islands though they may have coalesced into one island as they grew.

The three OBS massifs share many characteristics in terms of scenery and exposure. The successions consist of great accumulations of basaltic lavas, most between 0.5 and 4 m in thickness and consisting of a massive centre with rubbly tops and bottoms (e.g. stop 2.1); the successions also contain the remnants of numerous scoria cones. Most of the currently exposed lavas dip broadly seawards with angles between 10° and 30°, but this impression may be an artefact of the distribution of later cover. Having been exposed to subaerial erosion longer than other parts of Tenerife, the OBS terrains are deeply ravined, and this feature allows them to be easily distinguished from younger landscapes, even when now submerged below the sea (Figure 4a).

The subaerial OBS basalts constitute no more than a $1,000 - 2,000$ km^3 cap resting on a much larger volume of submarine basalt forming the foundation of the island, probably amounting to 15,000 to 20,000 km^3. The age range covered by this submarine component is unknown. This entire volume, including the sub-aerial part, constitutes the *shield-building phase* of the island. The bulk of it, predating the oldest dated subaerial lavas, probably consists of pillow lavas and **hyaloclastites** similar to those seen in Fuerteventura and La Palma.

Completion of the basaltic shield-building phase was followed by a period of volcanic repose and erosion that occurred from 4.2 to at least 3.5 Ma BP, producing a highly irregular erosional unconformity that is evident – picked out by differences in erosional style – in various parts of the island (e.g. around Santiago del Teide).

The Cañadas stratovolcano

The hiatus was followed by the construction of a new, large composite volcano, up to 40km in diameter, located at the junction between the three surviving OBS centres (Fig. 2) and rising at least 2,500m above the basaltic basement. This compositionally more diverse 'Cañadas volcano' probably grew to an overall volume of some 350-400km^3. Its development can be visualized as taking place in two (possibly overlapping) stages:

1. *Constructional phase.* Eruption of large volumes of basaltic, trachytic and phonolitic lavas, breccias and pyroclastics gradually constructed a large **stratovolcano**. During this stage, the addition of newly erupted material to the volcano slopes outpaced erosion. The products of this earlier phase, now overlain by later deposits, are under-represented among the rocks exposed today; they are found only *(i)* in deep barrancos and water-service tunnels on the flanks (e.g. stop 4.1), *(ii)* around the caldera rim (in places where later deposits have been eroded away), and *(iii)* at the base of the succession exposed in the caldera-wall. Ablay and Kearey (2000) even suggest, from

gravity data, that an entire mafic volcano – the Boca Tauce volcano – may be concealed beneath the present Cañadas edifice.

2. *Caldera-forming phase.* As the volcano's increasing elevation made it harder for newly supplied magma to reach the surface, magma began instead to accumulate *within* and beneath the volcano, leading to the development of a large, high-level magma chamber. Slow cooling (over tens to hundreds of thousands of years) allowed **fractional crystallisation** to generate substantial volumes of highly **evolved** compositions rich in dissolved gases such as **phonolite** in the shallower parts of this reservoir system[4], which in time fed a series of very large, explosive pyroclastic eruptions, mantling the flanks of the volcano with successive blankets of phonolitic pyroclastic deposits. Each such eruption, by removing support from the roof of the shallow chamber, contributed to the multiphase subsidence of the Cañadas caldera that developed at the volcano summit.

It is generally agreed, from the age of the oldest rocks found in the caldera wall and elsewhere, that the construction of the Cañadas volcano began around 3.5 Ma ago, but the details of its subsequent development are still the subject of some debate. Martí *et al.* (1994), and Bryan *et al.* (1998) divided the Cañadas succession into two lithostratigraphic groups (broadly corresponding to the constructional and caldera-forming phases above), divided by an unconformity. Ancochea *et al.* (1999) and Huertas *et al.* (2002) have however proposed a more complex history of pyroclastic eruptions and caldera-forming events. In this Guide, we sidestep this controversy by concentrating on the most recent pyroclastic eruptions, which are the best exposed and understood – the Upper Group of Martí *et al.* (1994) and its distal equivalent, the Bandas del Sur Group of Brown *et al.* (2003), which are summarized in Table 2.

The Cordillera Dorsal
From 0.9 Ma onward in parallel with the later stages of the construction of the Cañadas volcano, from 0.9 Ma onward, extensive outpourings of basalt further to the northeast constructed a spine of hills (the Cordillera Dorsal) linking the developing Cañadas edifice to the older Anaga massif. The volume of this post-erosional basaltic activity amounts to 250-300 km³. Fúster *et al.* (1968) considered these basalts to be part of the Old Basaltic 'Series', but subsequent K-Ar dating suggests they are much younger

---

[4]*U-series geochronology (Hawkesworth et al. 2000) suggests that parental mafic magmas fractionated over periods of perhaps 250,000 years, probably in upper mantle or deep-crustal reservoirs 20-30km below the surface (Ablay et al. 1998), feeding intermediate magmas to shallower chambers 3-4km below the Cañadas summit where they fractionated to highly evolved phonolite over periods of hundreds of years.*

Table 2. Stratigraphy of the later development of the Cañadas volcano, based on exposures in the caldera wall (Martí et al., 1994) and in the Bandas del Sur (Brown et al., 2003; Bryan et al., 1998; Ancochea et al., 1990).

Caldera wall stratigraphy	Volcanic products (caldera wall)	Age range[1]	Bandas del Sur stratigraphy	Bandas del Sur pyroclastic formations[2] (pf=pumice fall, i=ignimbrite, lb=lithic breccia)	Stops at which each is seen	Age
Upper Group — Diego Hernandez Formation	Phonolitic non-welded ignimbrites interbedded with basaltic scoria beds	0.54 – 0.17 Ma	Cycle 3[3]	• Abrigo Fm (i,lb) • La Caleta Fm[4] (pf,i,lb) • Sabinita Fm (pf) • Poris Fm[5] (pf,i,lb) • Fasnia Fm[6] (pf,i) • Aldea Blanca pf (pf) Basalt lavas & scoria cones	5.1, 5.2 4.5, 5.2 4.7, 5.2 5.2	169 ± 1 ka[7] 221 ± 5 ka[7] 275 ± 5 ka[7] 289 ± 6 ka[7]
Guajara Formation	Porphyritic phonolitic lavas and pyroclastics (including thick welded beds). Basaltic scoria beds at base	0.85 – 0.65 Ma	**Bandas del Sur Group**[2] Cycle 2	• Granadilla Fm (pf,i,lb) • Abades Fm (i) Lavas • Arico Fm[8] (pf,i,lb) Basalt lavas & scoria cones	4.2, 4.3 4.4, 4.6, 4.8,	600 ± 7 ka[7] 596 ± 14 ka[9] 668 ± 4 ka[7]
Ucanca Formation	Phonolite lavas and pyroclastics (including thick welded beds)	1.54 – 1.14 Ma	Cycle 1	• Eras Fm (pf,i)	W, N flanks + Las Eras	
Lower Group		3.3 – 2.0 Ma		Basalt, trachybasalt, trachyte and phonolite lavas	4.1	

[1] K-Ar ages by Martí et al (1994)
[2] Lithostratigraphy after Brown et al (2003). Many of the formations listed here were originally designated as Members by Bryan et al (1998).
[3] Divisions of Bryan et al (1998).
[4] Includes the Wavy Deposit of Bryan et al (1998).
[5] Includes the La Mareta Ignimbrite, Caldera del Rey Ignimbrite and Upper Grey Ignimbrite members of Bryan et al (1998).
[6] The Lower Grey Member of Bryan et al (1998).
[7] Ar-Ar age by Brown et al (2003).
[8] Includes as an unwelded lateral variant the Saltadero ignimbrite of Bryan et al (1998).
[9] K-Ar age reported by Bryan et al (1998).

(Table 1). Ancochea *et al*. (1990) attribute most of this 'Dorsal Series' to a narrow time slot between 0.9 ad 0.8 Ma, but in reality there may be no sharp chronological distinction between the constructional volcanic activity that formed the Dorsal edifice and the many pre-historic and historic basaltic eruptions that have since taken place here (*eg* Montaña de las Arenas and Montaña de la Negra on the Cordillera Dorsal, and Montaña de los Guirres and Montaña Grande in the Guimar valley) and elsewhere. One may therefore consider the 'Dorsal' volcanic episode to be still in progress.

Landslide valleys

Two prominent valleys have been excavated out of the Cordillera Dorsal at its junction with the Cañadas volcano. One hosts the town of Güimar near the east coast, and the other surrounds the town of La Orotava on the north coast (Figure 1). Both valleys are said to be floored by chaotic volcaniclastic breccia (*cf*. Stop 9.2), and are therefore considered to be the result of huge landslides, examples of '**sector collapse**' of the volcanic edifice occurring at some time between 0.87 and 0.29 Ma ago (Ancochea *et al*. 1990; Brown *et al*. 2003). The material removed from these col-

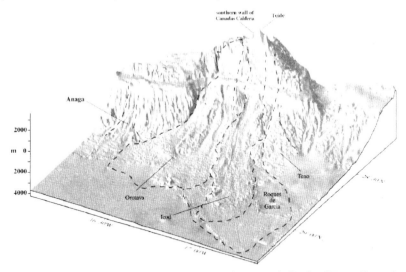

Figure 4a. Computer generated 3D image of the north flank of Tenerife and viewed from the northwest, showing topography above and below sea-level. The submarine topography is based on sidescan sonar data; sea-level is indicated by the diffuse horizontal band, representing inshore water depths too shallow to allow sonar scanning. The image (reproduced with permission from Masson et al. 2002, fig.17) clearly shows the morphological difference between deeply ravined areas of stable slope and rougher blocky surfaces of the debris avalanche deposits.

The volcanic evolution of Tenerife

lapse embayments can be traced as bathymetric highs directly offshore from each valley, and fans of acoustically 'hummocky' landslide deposit have been detected by sonar surveys to much greater distances (Watts & Masson, 1995; Krastel *et al.* 2001). Comparatively little of the breccia remains in each valley floor, hidden beneath 150-600m of younger volcanic rocks. The walls of these valleys expose the internal structure of the Dorsal volcanic pile from which they have been carved, which is most accessible for study in the southern wall of the Güimar valley (stop 5.3).

Sonar side-scan studies (Watts & Masson, 1995; Teide Group, 1997; Masson *et al.* 2002) indicate that the deposits from these topographically obvious landslide scarps are smaller in volume than multiple avalanche deposits derived from the steep northern slopes of the Cañadas edifice (Figure 4a and b), including the Icod valley. The total

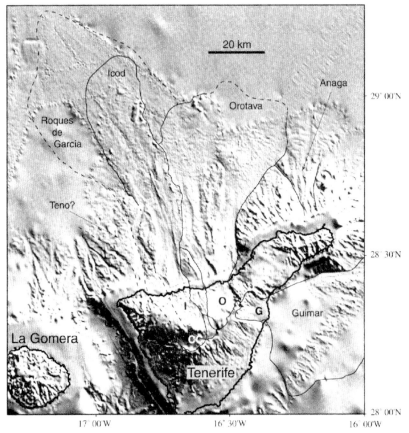

Figure 4b. Shaded relief map of Tenerife and surrounding sea floor, showing the extent of landslide/debris avalanche deposits around Tenerife (reproduced with permission of Elsevier from Masson et al 2002 fig. 6).

volume of submarine avalanche deposits around Tenerife is estimated to be in excess of 1000km^3, illustrating the enormous scale of mass wastage that may occur during the life of a typical volcanic oceanic island. Masson *et al.* (2002) consider that most Canary Island landslides were emplaced by sudden catastropic failure events (debris avalanches) rather than slow-moving creep processes, and the potential for generating damaging giant tsunamis[5] and their impact on distant coastlines has to be weighed in any assessment of volcanic risk associated with Tenerife and the other Canary Islands. When the Cumbre Viejo volcano on the neighbouring island of La Palma erupted in 1949, a large portion of its west flank slipped 4m towards the sea but then became locked (Keating & McGuire, 2000). This unstable block seems destined in due course to become the next debris avalanche deposit on the Canarian sea floor.

The caldera of Las Cañadas[6]

Between about 1.5 Ma and 0.17 Ma ago, the summit of the Cañadas volcano collapsed in stages (Martí *et al.* 1994; Brown *et al.* 2003) to form the dramatic elliptical depression known as the Caldera de Las Cañadas. The great German geologist Leopold von Buch visited Tenerife in 1815, and it was he who, on visiting Las Cañadas, first introduced the Spanish word '**caldera**' into the geological vocabulary. The magnificent walls that bound the caldera on its NE, E, SE and S margins, and the record of Cañadas edifice volcanism that they expose, constitute the most distinctive structural feature of the island. In plan view, these walls consist of a series of scallops (Figure 23). A large spur jutting out into the caldera – the Roques de Garcia – divides the caldera into two sectors with a difference in elevation of 150m and apparently different subsidence histories. The elevation difference between the present caldera floor and rim (on average ~600m) and the thickness of post-caldera volcanic rocks lying within the caldera (at least 500m) suggest a total subsidence of at least 1100 m (Martí *et al.* 1997). Multiplying this figure by the surface area of the caldera (a 16 x 9km^2 ellipse) provides a crude estimate of the volume of 'missing' material whose disappearance has to be accounted for: this estimate comes to about 125km^3. (Such estimates assume a uniform degree of subsidence across the caldera.)

The caldera fill in the SW sector at the present time consists mainly of lavas that have cascaded down from summit eruptions of Teide and Pico Viejo (see lower dia-

---

[5] *Visit www.bbc.co.uk/science/horizon/2000/mega_tsunami_transcript.shtml*
[6]*The term 'cañada' means 'grazing' and originates from the pre-Hispanic Guanche tradition of driving herds of goats from one side of the island to the other via the caldera at certain times of year, grazing them en route on the abundant broom that is still the dominant flora in the caldera. This practice continued until the first half of the twentieth century. More information on Tenerife history can be found in the small museum attached to the Parador hotel in the caldera.*

Table 3: Current hypotheses for the formation of the Caldera de Las Cañadas on Tenerife

	1. Multicyclic collapse caldera related to large-scale pyroclastic eruptions ('vertical collapse')	2. Multistage landslide depression related to successive episodes of flank failure ('lateral collapse')
Cartoon representation Each process is shown as single-stage for simplicity, but is actually multi-stage.		
Cause of subsidence of caldera floor	The caldera formed by progressive *vertical* collapse of the summit of the Cañadas volcano, associated with large-scale pyroclastic eruptions. By ejecting magma from large magma chambers immediately beneath the summit, they removed roof support leading to progressive subsidence.	The caldera depression and its topographic wall (most pronounced on the E, SE and S sides) formed as a result of progressive *lateral* collapse of the Cañadas edifice, caused by major landslides/debris avalanches that have taken place on the northern flank of the island.
Nature of the prominent arcuate caldera wall on the eastern, south-eastern and southern margins	The wall represents the eroded margin of the arcuate ring fault system that accommodated roof subsidence, *ie* a **topographic caldera margin**. (Repeated sector collapse of the N flank of Tenerife is largely incidental in this model.)	The scarp represents a series of headwall scars (getting younger from SW to NE) left behind after successive episodes of sector collapse/landsliding on the northern slopes of the island (recorded in their deposits offshore).
Geological observations that support the model, or which it explains	Much of the NE sector of the caldera wall has been removed by the La Orotava valley landslide scar, but a S-facing remnant survives at La Fortaleza (Excursion 6.6A), capped by welded proximal plinian fallout deposits similar to those seen along other sectors of the caldera rim (suggesting ring-fracture-controlled vents). Dyke intrusion patterns are also consistent with a vertical collapse caldera (Marti *et al* 1994). Brown *et al* (2003) consider it unlikely that Las Cañadas could have erupted >> 130 km³ **DRE** of pyroclastic products *without* undergoing caldera subsidence.	Proponents point to the lack of a continuous N and NW sector of the caldera wall. It is also known that ~1000 km³ of submarine avalanche deposits cover the sea floor north of Tenerife (Masson *et al* 2000). Proponents of lateral collapse argue that a large proportion of this was shed during three successive collapses of the north coast of Tenerife, which together led to formation of the *caldera-like* Las Cañadas lateral-collapse structure.
Main proponents	Ridley (1972), Booth (1973), Marti *et al* (1994, 1995, 1997), Bryan *et al* (1998), Hürlimann *et al* (1999) and Brown *et al* (2003).	Recent English-language summaries include Ancochea *et al* (1990, 1998, 1999), Cantagrel *et al* (1999), Carracedo (1994) and Masson *et al* (2002).

gram, back cover). The NE sector has been filled chiefly by products of several intra-caldera vents such as Montaña Blanca, Montaña Rajada and El Malpais de Sanatorio (Figure 23), with only a relatively minor contribution from Teide.

The mechanism by which the Caldera de Las Cañadas and its striking arcuate wall were formed has been a matter of dispute for decades (see Fuster *et al.* 1968, p.177). The current debate centres on two opposing hypotheses that are elaborated in Table 3. Several observations need to be taken into account in assessing the merits of each model. Firstly the prominent arcuate walls that so clearly define the caldera margin are present only on its eastern, south-eastern and southern sectors: no comparable topographic feature can be traced continuously across the north and west sides, although a remnant of (south-facing) northern caldera wall is preserved at La Fortaleza and El Cabezón (Excursion 6.6A; Figure 23). The supposed lack of a northern caldera wall has been a major plank in the case for the lateral collapse hypothesis since this asymmetry would be a predictable outcome of NNW-directed lateral collapse (Table 3), but opponents point out that an equivalent caldera ring-fault scarp existing to the north and north-west would have been (a) partially removed by sector collapse of the Orotava valley and (b) buried beneath the younger lavas of the Pico Viejo-Teide-Montaña Blanca/Rajada edifices, to which there is no equivalent in the eastern and southern sectors. Moreover, many vertical collapse calderas around the world have developed asymmetrically, and hinged patterns of subsidence are not uncommon. In the words of Brown *et al.* (2003), the present caldera 'resembles a breached ellipse rather than a typical sector-collapse horseshoe', and its topography is most easily interpreted as the product of vertical collapses, modified by various episodes of sector collapse and the construction of the Teide-Pico Viejo edifice.

Martí *et al.* (1994) argue that caldera formation occurred in three episodes with the focus shifting progressively from SW to NE, each episode associated with a major cycle of explosive pyroclastic eruptions: the Ucanca, Guajara and Diego Hernandez formations of the caldera wall. However, Brown *et al.* (2003) have questioned this association and suggest instead that numerous caldera collapse events were probably involved in producing the **nested** caldera structure seen today.

Basaltic flank eruptions

Throughout the development of the Cañadas edifice and caldera, which evidently entailed a succession of large evolved magma chambers beneath the centre of Tenerife, basalts, ankaramites and basanites have been erupting from numerous vents across the post-OBS flanks of the island. Several localities in this guide illustrate flank basalt scoria overlain by Bandas del Sur pyroclastics (*e.g.* Day 4 before Stop 4.1). Many of the more recent eruptions are represented by topographically well preserved mono-genetic scoria cones, numerous examples of which are easily seen while driving along the TF-1 motorway. Many are aligned along evident fissure traces (e.g. Figure 11 and Stop 7.2; see also Bryan *et al.* 1998 fig. 12). The volume of individual eruptions is small but their cumulative effect has been to cover significant areas of the island flanks with basaltic scoria and lavas flows.

Fúster *et al.* (1968) attempted to divide the flank basalts into 'Series III' and 'Recent' basalts on the basis of their degree of preservation, but the stratigraphic validity of such a distinction is doubtful as it seems clear that flank basalts have been erupting continually throughout the Cañadas and post-caldera history of the island.

Teide and Pico Viejo

The soaring stratocone of Teide (3718m) with its lower neighbour Pico Viejo (3103m) and various satellite vents constitute the post-caldera 'Teide-Pico Viejo (T-PV) complex', a large edifice constructed on the northern half of the caldera floor, consisting of basanite, trachyte and phonolite lavas (the inappropriately named 'Recent Acidic Series' of Fúster *et al.* 1968). This edifice has obliterated any caldera wall that existed there: its northern slopes plunge uninterrupted to the sea and have undergone sector failure to form the Icod valley (Figure 1). Teide and Pico Viejo share a common foundation of basic lavas, upon which each has built its own superstructure of intermediate to felsic lavas and pyroclastics that have evolved along geochemically distinct magmatic lineages (the Pico Viejo and Pico Teide magma series of Ablay *et al.* 1998). The current summit of Teide, El Pitón, sits within **nested** craters that record the destruction of at least two earlier summit cones (Martí *et al.* 1995). The most recent output of Teide consists of summit-fed richly feldspar-phyric vitric phonolite flows which form prominent levéed features on its southern and eastern flanks (see front cover). Though the T-PV complex is usually regarded as stratigraphically distinct from the Cañadas succession, it is likely that its present appearance differs little from that of the Cañadas volcano prior to caldera collapse.

Several satellite vents are associated with the T-PV edifice, notably the lava dome centres of Montaña Blanca and Montaña Rajada that have constructed a prominent shoulder on the eastern flank of Teide (front cover). Rather surprisingly the magmatic development of this centre has been closely tied in with that of Pico Viejo rather than Teide (Ablay *et al.* 1998). The most recent event here was a compound lava and sub-plinian pyroclastic eruption with late dome-forming lava effusion that took place about 2000 years ago, synchronously with similar activity on Pico Viejo. Subsequent T-PV activity has reverted to Teide summit eruptions.

Historic eruptions

Post-Montaña Blanca historic basanite eruptions have occurred in 1430, 1704-5, 1706, 1798 and 1909 (Cabrera-Lagunilla & Hernández-Pacheco, 1989) in three parts of the island:
1. An alignment of vents at a low elevation in the vicinity of Puerto de la Cruz in 1430 AD (Montañas de la Horca, de los Frailes and de Gañanias – see Stop 9.2).

2. At the SW end of the Cordillera Dorsal in 1704-5 AD (Montaña Arenas, Volcán de Fasnia and Volcán Siete Fuentes – see Stops 5.4, 5.9 and 5.12).
3. In the volcanic zone sometimes referred to as the Santiago Rift linking Pico Viejo and the Teno massif (Montaña Negra/Garachico in 1706 AD, Chahorra/Narices del Teide in 1798 AD and Chinyero in 1909 – see Stop 2.8, Excursion 8.3 and Stops 8.4 and 8.6). The explosion pit in the Pico Viejo caldera is also believed to have formed in 1798.

Itineraries

To cater for all tastes and degrees of mobility, we have included in this Guide more stops than can practicably be covered in a 7-day visit, and therefore users will need to be selective in the stops they choose to visit. To aid the visitor with limited time, the localities in this itinerary are graded according to geological significance: three-star localities (***) may be considered essential for a representative grasp of Tenerife geology, the others optional according to time and inclination. Off-road walks are also graded for access: '3-volcano' (^^^) excursions are the least accessible or require the most physical fitness or agility; the elderly or less fit should give these a miss. Note that the itinerary for Day 7 consists of a single long walk, and readers not wishing to undertake this will have a day in hand for other localities. Day 8 offers two alternative walks which cannot both be completed in one day.

The visitor's attention is again drawn to the important safety considerations listed on pp 3-4.

Days 1-3. Old Basalts of the Roque del Conde, Teno and Anaga Massifs

The Neogene Old Basalt 'Series' of Fúster *et al*. (1968), the subaerial manifestation of Tenerife's early shield-building stage, can be seen in imposing mountain massifs at, or near to, each apex of the triangular island (Figure 1):

- El Roque del Conde ("The Count's Castle") massif near Adeje in the south.
- the Teno massif in the west.
- the Anaga massif north of Santa Cruz in the extreme northeast.

Basalt enthusiasts and ocean island aficionados may want to visit all three of these centres to compare their individual characteristics, but anyone whose visit is confined to a week will find one or two of them sufficient. The Anaga massif is commonly cloudier and wetter than the rest of the island, the basalts there are more deeply weathered, and a visit will entail a longer drive from resorts in the south of the island; nonetheless the spectacular scenery there is undoubtedly worth a visit in spite of its remoteness.

Day 1. Roque del Conde massif (southern Tenerife)

The Roque del Conde area, readily accessible from the main airport (Reina Sofia) in the south of the island, provides two convenient half-day excursions, either of which could be tackled after an early inward flight or before a late return flight. About 1000m of Roque del Conde basalts is exposed in the Barranco del Infierno (Hell's Gorge) near to Adeje (Excursion 1.1). Recent **Ar-Ar dating** (Table 1) suggests at least part of the sequence was erupted about 11.3 Ma ago, significantly earlier than previous K-Ar dates of 6-8 Ma (Ancochea et al. 1990) implied. The new age data also suggest that the Roque del Conde succession is substantially older than the other two subaerial massifs (Table 1). The sequence is chemically and isotopically fairly uniform, being dominated in the lower parts by alkali basalt and in the upper parts by hawaiite (Thirlwall et al. 2000).

Excursion 1.1: Adeje and the Barranco[7] del Infierno *** ∧

Follow the TF-1 motorway north from Playa de las Americas and take the first exit signed to Adeje. A prominent low-altitude ridge with a cross on top just before the turn-off is composed of 2-3 **mugearite** flows. In Adeje, take the one-way system upward following sparse signs for 'Infierno', up to the top of the town (Figure 5(a)), and park[8] on a steep road near to the Mirador[9] and the Restaurant Otello (specializing in garlic chicken). On the opposite (SE) wall of the valley can be seen a typical succession of the Old Basaltic 'Series', comprising thin flows with rubbly tops that dip gently to the south (Figure 6). The trail begins below the mirador and initially follows the northwest wall of the barranco. Here it traverses two evolved ignimbrite units separated by an ash bed, a prominent pumice fall bed and overlying lavas, cut by several dykes. These evolved pyroclastics, topographically lower than a substantial thickness of Older Basalts, were viewed by Neumann et al. (1999) as part of the OBS succession itself, but they can be traced down to the west coast, where feldspars from a similar ignimbrite have given an Ar-Ar age of 1.4 Ma (C-A Craig, unpublished PhD thesis, University of London 2003) suggesting that the pyroclastics here belong to the Cañadas succession and were deposited in a palaeovalley cut into the OBS.

The path descends to the barranco floor around an area signposted La

---

[7] 'Barranco' means a deep ravine.
[8] Facing downhill is recommended (leave in gear, chock wheels).
[9] 'Mirador' means a panoramic viewing point.

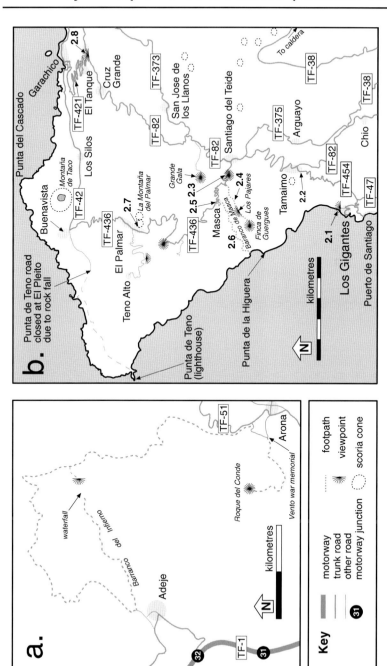

Figure 5. Sketch map showing localities in the (a) Roque del Conde and (b) Teno massifs.

Day 1. Roque del Conde massif (southern Tenerife)

Figure 6. Thin flows of Old Basalt 'Series' in the Barranco del Infierno. (Excursion 1.1) Note the weakly jointed thicker (ponded) flow in the cliff above the figures.

Cojadera (*ca.* 30min. walk from parking). The southeastern wall opposite (Figure 6) shows a typical part of the succession, comprising thin flows dipping seaward, with occasional reddish soil horizons marking short pauses in volcanic output; the succession is cut by occasional dykes and intrusive sheets. A somewhat thicker, indistinctly jointed hawaiite flow can be seen directly above the lowest soil horizon. Continuing into the upper gorge, exposures of basalt flows become near-continuous along the path. The flows are quite fresh and include both weakly olivine phyric basalts and occasional phenocryst-rich ankaramites. Flow thickness ranges from 50cm to 3-4m, and the flows often have rubbly bottoms. The trail ends at a waterfall.

Excursion 1.2: Roque del Conde from Arona ** ^^

An alternative overview of this OBS massif and the south of the island can be had by climbing Roque del Conde itself (1001m), by the path leading from the hamlet of Vento (650m) near Arona. From the south coast, take the TF-28 from autopista Junction 27 to La Camella, then the TF-51 to Arona. Turn left in Arona, continuing up the TF-51, but turning left by a phone box after 250m. Park near the war memorial/roundabout 500m along this road, from where signs point to the Roque del Conde trail. If approaching from Vilaflor, turn right off the TF-51 just after km post 5, which leads to the same monument.

The upper part of the Roque del Conde succession can also be accessed by driving further up the TF-51, turning left toward Ifonche and parking at the end of the paved road. A track leaves here for the col between Roque Imoque and Roque de los Brezos. The volcanics here are mostly weakly plagioclase-phyric hawaiite and mugearite.

Day 2. Teno massif (western Tenerife)

Ancochea *et al.* (1990) divided the Teno stratigraphy into a lower succession of seaward-dipping basalts (interbedded with pyroclastics and volcaniclastics), unconformably overlain by flatter-lying basalt lavas interspersed with trachyte. Though a sharp transition from seaward-dipping to flat-lying flows is seen in places (e.g. Locality 2.3), there is little evidence of a major unconformity dividing the Teno succession as a whole. Moreover, the correlation of lava geochemistry with stratigraphy, together with the small difference in Ar-Ar ages (6.4 – 6.0 Ma) between the lower and uppermost parts of the succession, suggests that the Teno pile represents a single magmatic cycle (Thirlwall *et al.* 2000).

Take the motorway northwest from Playa de las Americas, leaving at the second exit labelled Adeje. Instead of turning right into Adeje, turn left on to the coast road signed to San Juan. *All km readings for Day 2 are from this exit.* Note the island of La Gomera (a basaltic shield volcano, the only island in the Canaries showing no Quaternary volcanism) straight ahead. The topographic contrast between the gently seaward-dipping slopes of the Cañadas volcano across which the road runs and the rugged Teno massif ahead becomes clearer as one progresses northwest. At 11.9 km, follow signs to Puerto Santiago and Los Gigantes. Turn left at 19.3 km (same signing). Filter right at 20.1 km into the town of Los Gigantes (Figure 5(b)). Continue downhill and turn right up Calle Tabaiba. Park just before a rightward bend and roadcut in the road overlooking the sea.

Stop 2.1 (21.6 km): Los Gigantes *** ∧

Walk along a rough track on the left, leading north. The end of the track overlooks the sea and offers a magnificent panorama (Figure 7) across to the vertical sea cliffs of the Teno massif as far as Punta de la Higuera. Observe the following features:
(a) a 600m-thick succession of relatively thin, grey basalt flows (most 1-3m thick); where exposed in three dimensions, the flows can be seen to dip gently seaward (5-15° to SW).
(b) the flows are cut by numerous thin vertical northerly-striking dykes; some are truncated at various heights up the cliff and may have fed surface flows at these elevations, while others appear to extend to the top of the cliff.
(c) brown triangular features showing local outward-dipping bedding that appear to be scoria cones dissected by the cliff face (Figure 7). One draped by a prominent yellow weathered scoria bed is the most obvious; a flow covering this is truncated by a later cone that has developed on the shoulder of the first. A third, less distinct

Figure 7. Annotated view NNW from Los Gigantes showing the lower part of the Teno basalt succession (Stop 2.1)

cone is exposed lower in the succession to the NW.

The cliffs provide dramatic evidence of the 'debuttressing' effect of wave action, which makes all oceanic islands susceptible to structural failure and **sector collapse**.

Turning back towards the road, the lavas exposed by the track are weakly porphyritic **transitional** alkali basalts, but clasts of ankaramite in a calcreted scree here suggest the presence of ankaramite lavas higher up in the succession. Note the small greenish xenoliths (either olivine cumulates formed at crustal depths or perhaps mantle **harzburgites**) exposed in a flow near the start of the path. The structure of the individual lavas can be examined by walking a few metres up the road, where a roadcut exposes an alternation of massive centres and rubbly **a'a** flow-tops (the latter doubtless including rubbly material incorporated into the base of the succeeding flow - it is generally not possible to distinguish here between rubbly tops and rubbly bottoms). Near the top of the cut a yellowish soil horizon can be seen, marking a break in lava eruption.

Turn the car round, and re-join the one-way traffic system in Los Gigantes, turning left at a T-junction (22.3km), filtering left at 22.5 km, and turning left again at the top of a hill (22.8km), signed to Santiago del Teide. The road proceeds up a valley between two cliffs of OBS basalts, but the valley is floored by younger lavas (Figure 1). As you enter Tamaimo, park on the right of the road by a café.

Stop 2.2 (28.2km): Edge of Tamaimo *

Looking upward and westward to the cliffs beyond the road, a dissected, well jointed ponded lava flow can be seen, surrounded by the remnants of a scoria cone against which higher flows appear to be banked.

Continue into Tamaimo and turn left at the T-junction (29.9km) on the (TF-82). At Santiago del Teide (36.9km) take the left turn signed to Masca-Buenavista (TF-436), just before a grey and white church. The road winds up to a pass, where cars may be parked on either side of the road. *Pay attention to constant traffic on this narrow road*.

Stop 2.3 (38.3km): Pass above Santiago del Teide ***

The pass (often with a convenient refreshment kiosk) provides excellent views of typical rugged OBS topography. Note the contrast in erosional style with the gentler slopes of the Cañadas edifice to the southeast. On a bearing of 310°, one can see an abrupt transition between the seaward-dipping lower part of the Teno basalt sequence to the west and flatter-lying upper lavas to the east. In the 1318m peak that overlooks the mirador to the north, late **trachytic** dykes can be seen cutting well jointed, flat-lying upper sequence basalt flows, with paler, more **evolved** flows capping the summit. On a bearing of 208° can be seen a pale trachytic stock (Roque

Day 2. Teno massif (western Tenerife)

Blanco) representing a late intrusion of the same evolved magma.

Those wishing to undertake further investigations on foot may choose between two alternatives (Excursions 2.4 and 2.6); it is not feasible to attempt both in the same day.

Excursion 2.4 (39.3 km): Ridge walk to Los Pajares (1034m) *** ^^

From the pass, the road descends to another parking place on the right (39.3km), shortly before the road swings sharply to the right a round a breezeblock hut; parking may be difficult here after midday.

To walk along the ridge to Los Pajares (1034m, ~1 hour each way) and Finca de Guergue beyond, walk 50m down the road to a left turn on the outside of the right bend, closed by a cable with a sign saying 'Privado No Pasar No Trespassing'. Proceed 25m down this track then take a turn on the right clearly marked by a wooden arrow saying 'Finca de Gerge' (sic). This cairned and paved path (+ red paint spots) leads up and down the ridge to a gate in a fence and then ascends up to Los Pajares peak. Note the rubbly lavas of ankaramite and basalt, cut by numerous dykes of ankaramite, hawaiite and mugearite trending 355°-020°. Across the main valley can be seen massively jointed horizontal flows of the upper Teno OBS succession, also cut by numerous N-S dykes. Possible structural controls on this prevailing dyke trend can be discussed[10]. As the path descends to the gate beneath vertically jointed flows, look out for yellow-weathering ultramafic xenoliths in the basalts across which the path leads.

The summit of Los Pajares offers impressive views to La Gomera and El Hierro, and a panorama across the Barranco de Masca. To the north can be seen the steep junction between, on the left, older Teno flows dipping at 15° toward the coast and, to the right, horizontal flows of younger Teno basalts and more evolved magmas (Figure 8a). Though an unconformity must exist between these older and younger lava groups, it seems more likely that the steep boundary between them here is a N-S normal fault passing through Masca village below.

Return to the carpark, noting that some flows along this ridge dip seaward while others seem to be flat-lying: how are they related? Continue down the TF-436 to Masca village, parking as close as possible to the roundabout.

Stop 2.5 (42.8 km): Masca carpark ***

The carpark on its NE side is cut into rubbly ankaramite lavas cut by dykes. Beneath a prominent palm tree overlooking a one-way section of road can be seen

---

[10] *This prevailing trend is at odds with the suggestion of a NW-SE-trending rift in the Teno peninsula (cf. Carracedo and Day, 2002 Figure 1.3).*

Figure 8a. Thin phenocryst-rich ankaramite flows in Masca village (Stop 2.5).

a

Figure 8b. Pahoehoe toes in basalts of the lower Barranco de Masca. Water bottle 20 cm high for scale (Excursion 2.6).

Figure 8c. Teno OBS succession above Playa de Masca (Excursion 2.6)

series of unusually thin (~20cm thick) lava flows, with glassy tops sometimes showing **pahoehoe** wrinkles in cross-secton, whose lower halves are very densely charged with clinopyroxene and olivine phenocrysts (Fig. 8a). Though alkali basalt *melts* can be expected to have low viscosity on account of the high alkali content and relatively low silica, a **magma** containing such a high concentration of crystals would possess a significant yield strength and would flow only very slowly, so it is difficult to see how such thin, crystal-rich flows could be emplaced. One possible explanation is that, as they dip at about 25°, these 'flows' may merely be cumulate remnants of thicker, less crystal-rich lava flows that were sufficiently fluid for dense mafic phenocrysts to settle out as the lava flowed, to form a carpet at the base of the moving flow. The phenocryst-depleted upper portions of these flows may have continued to flow down-slope, leaving behind thin, less fluid, crystal-cumulate basal zones retaining only a veneer of the original magma.

Excursion 2.6: Barranco de Masca (from Stop 2.5) *** ^^^

For the energetic, the Barranco de Masca below offers an unparalleled cross-section of the internal architecture of a volcanic ocean island. The walk consists of two stages: the first stage down to the confluence of a side barranco (30 minutes down and 45 minutes back up), and a second optional stage down to the Playa de Masca at sea level (2h down from the road; allow at least 3h for the 600m/2000ft ascent back to road).

Descend to the left down steep paved tracks that begin just beyond the round-about, leading past a couple of restaurants. Near the end of the paved section as it levels out before the last buildings, turn left down a steep rough path descending into the barranco. Magnificent piles of thin pahoehoe lavas are seen during the first stage of the walk, cut by a relatively dense dyke swarm feeding higher flows. The lavas here are dominantly ankaramite, sometimes showing impressive concentrations of augite phenocrysts (samples of which can be recovered from the gravel in the path). In the fork above the dam, a whole cliff section appears to consist of thin (~20cm thick) ankaramite lavas cut by numerous dykes. Most of the lavas here are highly altered and unsuitable for isotopic dating, though one feldspar-phyric lava has yielded an Ar-Ar plagioclase mineral age of 6.4 Ma (Thirlwall *et al.* 2000).

After the dam, where a tributary valley joins from the right, the winding barranco becomes even more steep-sided and dramatic and a helmet is recommended, particularly after rain. The steep descent displays a profusion of seaward-dipping ankaramite and basalt lavas (pahoehoe and a'a style) cut by numerous dykes and gently dipping sheets, and even the occasional dissected scoria cone. Playa de Masca (Figure. 8c) offers swimming opportunities and views of La Gomera across a sparkling ocean. It is also a convenient destination for a boat trip from Los Gigantes. On the return walk to Masca, look out for thin pahoehoe lava-toes to the left of the track (Figure 8b), and a dissected scoria cone cut by two large dykes in a 180° bend in the gorge. Take care not to lose the path in places where it climbs out of the barranco bottom.

Day 2. Teno massif (western Tenerife)

Return to the road and drive in the direction of Buenavista. Typical examples of the higher parts of the Teno succession can be seen on the roadside northwest of Masca, in particular after the left turn marked to Los Carrizales. These are thicker flows, around 1-2m thick, and include both ankaramite and nearly aphyric lavas, both much fresher than the basalts in the barranco. Numerous N-S dykes again emphasise the importance of fissure eruptions in constructing ocean islands. To what extent does edifice failure determine the trend of such dykes?

The two following stops illustrate *post-Older-Basalt mafic eruptions*. Continuing on the Buenavista del Norte road over a second pass, a prominent pair of cinder cones (one radially dissected by quarrying) can be seen in the valley below, beside the village of El Palmar. After a right curve leading into the village, proceed 0.5km further and take the first side-road on the right, turning right again on to a back street running parallel to the main road. The entrance to the quarried scoria cone can be found on the left after a few tens of metres.

Stop 2.7 (53.6 km): La Montaña del Palmar scoria cone *** ∧

The quarrying, providing access to a deep radial cross-section of the cone, has exposed the zonation observed in a typical scoria cone between its central parts and the margins. The central part, deepest into the cut, is built of reddish scoria, oxidised by the sustained high temperatures close to the central vent (not exposed). The scoria lapilli are well sorted (characteristic of a fall deposit), grading from coarser in the interior to finer in the black (cooler) western margin. The beds dip outward, the dip picked out in places by less vesicular slabs, probably representing fragments of degassed skin that formed on the magma surface in the vent during less explosive phases (Cas and Wright, 1987, fig. 6.12) and were ejected by later explosions.

Continue down to the T-junction outside Buenavista (59.6 km). The left turn leads toward the lighthouse at Punta del Teno, but this magnificent cliff road has sadly been closed (at El Pleito) owing to hazardous rock-fall from the cliffs above[11]. Instead, turn right on the TF-42 through Los Silos, then turn right again at the outskirts of Garachico (the centre of which is worth a visit) up a winding road (initially TF-1421 then TF-421 but see Update 4 on p108) leading up through El Tanque village centre to the TF-82, noting poorly vegetated lava fields and lava levées across which the upper bends of the road traverse. At the T-junction, turn left and pull into a café/shop carpark.

Stop 2.8: Panorama of Garachico ***

Below the eastern end of the shop lies a splendid panorama of Garachico, a town

[11] The sign says 'Closed - proceed at own risk'.

Day 2. Teno massif (western Tenerife)

largely destroyed by the 1706 lava eruption from the cone of Montaña Negra, 6.5 km due south of - and 1300m above - the town (Figure 5); the course of this flow can be picked out on the Kompass map as an unvegetated strip running from Las Montañas Negras to Garachico. The town has been rebuilt on the 1706 lava apron formed as the lava, plunging down the cliff, reached the sea. The remnants of the steep lava flow and its levées, across which the ascending road zigzagged, can be clearly seen to the east of the carpark.

A fine retrospective panorama across the Teno massif is available from Grande Gala (1354m), reached by parking up a steep side-turning on the right (105.3km). From there you have to walk about 1.6km along a metalled road, climbing about 150m.

Return to southern resorts via TF-82 to Santiago del Teide, noting views of Pico del Teide *en route*. After Santiago the route via Arguayo is recommended (TF-375): it traverses a pass on an outlier of the Teno massif where thick mugearite, benmoreite and trachyte flows of the upper part of the Teno sequence may be observed.

Day 3. Anaga massif (northeastern Tenerife)

This part of the itinerary is listed here because it deals with an Older Basalt succession broadly similar to Days 1 and 2. Given its remoteness from the tourist resorts in the south, however, a visit to Anaga would more sensibly be undertaken toward the end of the trip from a base in San Cristobal de La Laguna (known simply as La Laguna) or Puerto de la Cruz. In scenic terms the area is as dramatic as Teno and well worth experiencing, but the geology is not that different (except for a higher proportion of evolved phonolitic lavas, plugs and dykes). The lavas are not as well exposed as in Teno owing to the lusher vegetation, and many basalt exposures are hydrothermally altered or deeply weathered. You may also experience poorer weather in Anaga than in other parts of the island. If only one day can be spent on the Older Basalt massifs, the one chosen should be Teno.

Fúster *et al.* (1968) divided the Anaga OBS succession into 3 formations which they believed to be separated by two unconformities. The most impressive sections in scenic terms are to be seen on the SE side of the Anaga peninsula; magnificent sections are seen along the road to San Andrés (TF-11) and in the cliffs beyond. Unlike Teno where ankaramite and alkali basalt predominate, the lower flows SW of San Andrés are nearly aphyric hawaiite and tephrite. Aphyric to ankaramitic alkali basalts predominate NE of San Andrés (along the TF-121 to Igueste de San Andrés), but ankaramites are relatively rare in Anaga as a whole. The stratigraphy is more clearly exposed on the northwest slope of the peninsula, in the Mesa de Tejina (northwest of La Laguna). Exposures along the magnificent Anaga ridge itself are heavily altered and deeply weathered.

Two alternative excursions are offered for an 'Anaga Day'; one on the SE coast aimed at serious walkers, and another to the north of the ridge better suited to the less energetic. The first begins at Igueste de San Andrés on the SE side of the peninsula and the second at the tiny hamlet of Afur (Figure 9).

Excursion 3.1: Walk to Playa de Antequera *** ^^^ [12]

Drive through Santa Cruz and San Andrés to Igueste de San Andrés (TF-121), a village some 7 km to the northeast of San Andrés, backed by hills covered with clumps of *Euphorbia canariensis* ('candelabra bush'). It may be helpful to pause by the bar (El Rincon de Igueste) at the start of the village to sketch the headland

---

[12] *Playa de Antequera is reported to be a nudist beach in the summer.*

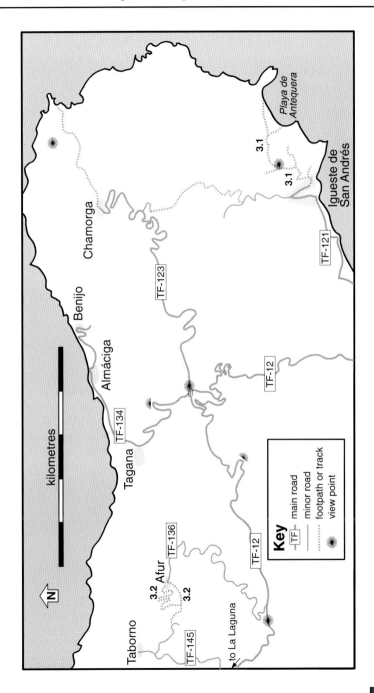

Figure 9.   Sketch Map showing localities in the Anaga Massif.

across the valley, which can be seen to consist of a lower scoria unit (orangey brown), a middle greyer unit of lavas dipping toward the sea, and another pile of scoria at the top of the ridge. Drive through Igueste to the older part of the village on the eastern side of the barranco. Park as close as possible to the bus stop at the end of the road.

Prepare for a 5-hour walk, and proceed past the church and toddlers' play area on the paved track that becomes the Paseo de Cemeteria leading to the walled village cemetery. Turn left just before a little bridge over a gully, on to an initially unimposing track marked by blue paint arrows; if you see 'No' in blue on the track you have missed the turn. The trail from here on has been hewn out of heavily weathered scoria, periodically cut by ankaramitic to intermediate dykes trending 125°. A sharp pinnacle on the left sits on an accumulation of orange-red, indurated scoria typical of this section of the hillside: it probably represents the flanks of a scoria cone now buried within the hillside beneath overlying lavas (of which the pinnacle itself mainly consists). Continue up the trail through deeply weathered seaward-dipping lavas. The longest straight section of path, however, runs alongside a very fresh grey feldspar-phyric **trachyte** lava about 2.5m thick; the base is rubbly where it rests on basaltic ash beneath, and the upper part is also rubbly with a marked upward increase in vesicularity. Scattered blue crystals of sodalite can just be seen on a fresh surface under a hand lens, as well as sparse dark alkali pyroxene phenocrysts.

This track leads eventually to the signal station. However, shortly before it levels out, two inconspicuous cairns (one each side of the trail) mark the start of a smaller track branching off on the left. Take this track, noting alternating beds of (i) lithic breccia (poorly sorted granular clasts of various kinds in a finer matrix) and (ii) scoria, beneath (iii) basaltic lava flows above the new track. These beds record (i) explosive interaction of ascending basaltic magma with ground- or surface-water, generating phreatomagmatic blasts, (ii) mildly explosive **strombolian** eruptions of basaltic magma following removal of the water barrier, and (iii) eruption of basaltic lava. These products may all derive from the same vent or fissure.

Continue along the track to the top of the ridge, passing over thick accumulations of dark lithic tuffs with basaltic **ballistics** of all sizes passing up into finer bedded ashes, suggesting further phreatomagmatic explosions. On reaching the ridge (cairn), turn left and walk up to a stone hut on the summit (430m). From here or the trig point nearby, there is a superb view of Anaga scenery to the N and NE. The valley leading to the Playa de Antequera lies directly below, and beyond it (bearing 060°) a hill is capped by remnants of a scoria cone (smooth 'felty' surface, red-orange colour). Further inland (340°), hills can be seen to be cut by a 120°-trending dyke swarm of light coloured **evolved** (probably trachytic) dykes, some of which form impressive positive features.

To get to the beach, walk toward the trig point but turn off to the left by a cairn. This path leads down the east side of the NNW-trending main ridge. As the

Figure 10. Section of a scoria cone with a weathered top overwhelmed by basaltic lavas in the Old Basalt 'Series' of the Anaga Massif, SW end of the Playa de Antequera, NE of Santa Cruz (Excursion 3.1). Figure gives scale.

descending path levels out across the head of the valley, take a path on the right (marked by another cairn) that descends more steeply toward the Punta de Antequera now in view. This cairned path winds down into the valley bottom and eventually crosses the watercourse. Take note of a white arrow pointing left at this point. Head roughly perpendicular to the watercourse (not to the right) and find a path a little way up the opposite valley side. Turn right and follow this path which leads round the spur towards dipping orange-brown beds of scoria above an over-hang. These beds form part of a scoria cone that has been covered by later lavas. To reach the main beach for a swim or to see a better cross-section of a scoria cone covered by OBS lavas, it is necessary to skirt around to the left (NE) to find another path at a higher level (becoming whitish further on). Alternatively, follow the original path directly down to reach a cove at the southern end of the bay (cut off from the main playa at high tide) where impressive dipping scoria beds with a pronounced weathered top can be seen (Figure 10). Climbing down to the cove shows the beds to be cut by two olivine-pyroxene-phyric basanite dykes .

From here one can look E across the bay to the Punta de Antequera where a well jointed, thick phonolite flow appears to overlie seaward-dipping basaltic lavas (unconformably, according to Fúster *et al*, 1968 fig. 38).

Returning to Igueste, take care not to lose the cairned path up the south side of the valley.

Excursion 3.2: Afur ** ^^

The alternative Anaga excursion begins on the TF-12 leading from La Laguna east-ward along the spine of the Anaga peninsula. The road passes the Mirador de Jardina (on the outside of a leftward bend just before km post 25) from where one has a good view back toward La Laguna, and can compare the deeply ravined OBS terrain in the foreground (and to left and right) with the smoother outlines of the Cañadas edifice beyond. Note the bifurcating 2m dyke in the angle of the bend. The Ermita Cruz del Carmen 2.5km further on (viewpoint at the far end of the carpark on the right) allows the same comparison, and has an interesting display board on hydrogeology; note also the Canary Palm (*Phoenix canariensis*) and the surrounding forest of laurel and tree heather typical of the Anaga ridge. 6.6km further (0.6km after km post 19), the road runs along the crest of the ridge with views to either side. Take the left turn signed to Afur (TF-136) and *set the trip recorder to 0.0 here*.

After 1.0km on a right hand bend note lavas with vesicular tops and bottoms. At 2.0 km, one can see a large mass of trachyte, probably a lava dome, on the hill-side ahead. At 2.2 km one can examine well sorted basaltic scoria interbedded with finer ash cut by several dykes trending 060°; a side-turn here leads to crags of the trachyte body viewed from across the valley. A large carpark is available in Afur, at the end of the metalled road.

From the western end of the carpark, take a dirt track signed to Taborno.

Day 3. Anaga massif (northeastern Tenerife)

Much of the solid rock exposed in the extensively terraced hillside ahead (bearing 240° - it may be helpful to make a sketch here) consists of dykes cutting the basalt succession, which on this side of the peninsula is deeply weathered and poorly exposed. As the track swings southward down into the valley bottom, note a 15m-thick feldspar-phyric trachyte dyke to the left of the track, which extends as light-coloured slabs up the hillside opposite. Looking back from the other side of the barranco where the track zig-zags up through cultivated terraces, it is clear that this dyke forms the 070°-trending rocky rib on which the village of Afur has been built, traceable up into the hillside beyond toward Roque El Fraile. The track passes low exposures of rotten basalt lava cut by more dykes trending roughly E-W. As the track climbs up toward a hamlet, the abundance of E-W dykes becomes ever more apparent; from track-side exposures some are basic (ankaramite) but many are more evolved in composition (trachybasalt and trachyte). On a bearing of 032° a dissected scoria cone can be seen cut by a prominent dyke.

On arriving in the upper hamlet, the track to Taborno may be followed to the top of the hillside, where fresh flows of trachyte will be seen capping the basalts along the side of the metalled road to Taborno. A shorter alternative is to turn left down the paved pedestrian track directly back to Afur. Before leaving the hamlet, look up to the SE to see again the prominent pale crag formed by the trachyte dome noted from the road. Many more dykes can be seen on the hillside directly south. Descending the paved track, the jointing seen in the southern wall of the Afur dyke dips surprisingly steeply, suggesting[13] that this dyke in places has a complex shape with a relatively shallow dipping southern contact. Where the cement path climbs up to the village after two footbridges, it zig-zags several times across the contact (here quite steep) between this dyke and the rubbly brecciated basalt lava into which it was intruded. The Bar Jose Canon provides refreshments. Return to base up the TF-136 and TF-12.

---

[13] *Columnar jointing forms perpendicular to a cooling surface. The jointing in a dyke with vertical contacts (ie vertical cooling surfaces) is therefore normally sub-horizontal.*

Day 4. The Cañadas succession in the 'Bandas del Sur' area

Following the close of OBS shield-building eruptions, a new central volcanic edifice, erupting a larger proportion of evolved volcanic products, was constructed on the eroded OBS basement between 3.2 and 0.17 Ma ago. Day 4 (Figure 11) is devoted to the rocks of this 'Cañadas volcano', including the 'Granadilla **pumice**' of Booth (1973). Localities 4.1 to 4.4 all lie along the TF-28 high-level road between San Miguel and Arico.

Take exit 24 from the Autopista del Sur signed to San Miguel, Los Abrigos and Las Galletas. *Kilometre distances for today's localities are measured from this exit.* Proceed north along the TF-65 toward San Miguel. At 2.7km, note a quarry on the right extracting scoria from a cone that is overlain by Bandas del Sur fall and ignimbrite deposits. This emphasises the fact that flank basalt eruptions were taking place throughout the construction of the Cañadas edifice.

At 9.0 km, turn right on to TF-28, leave San Miguel and stop on the left hand side immediately after a bridge over a deep gorge called the Barranco de la Orchilla at 10.9 km.

Stop 4.1 (10.9 km): Trachyphonolite lava dome beside T-28 road where it crosses Barranco de la Orchilla **

The barranco cuts a 100m-thick pale **trachyte** lava that Fúster et al. (1968) attributed to the lower part of the exposed Cañadas succession (Table 2)[14]. Phenocrysts of alkali feldspar and amphibole are visible, but the rock is otherwise undistinctive. The crudely columnar-jointed sheet appears to consist of at least three flow units; one internal contact, dipping to the NE, can be seen above the SW end of the bridge where an upper flow unit chills against the one below; a second can be seen high in the face forming the NE side of the barranco. Walking back up the road, flow-banding bearing witness to local magma mixing can be seen on the upper E side of the road-cut. This lava pinches out quite rapidly as one walks further to the SW, suggesting a lensoid cross-section for the compound lava body, probably filling a palaeovalley. It is overlain (up the barranco) by a scoria cone from which a basic lava has erupted.

At the NE end of the bridge, the trachyte lava is cut by an olivine basalt dyke

---

[14] *An inevitable consequence of the **constructional** phase of a volcano is that much of the earlier stages of growth remain hidden in the interior of the volcano and are under-represented in any stratigraphy based on surface mapping.*

whose irregular course seems to have been determined by pre-existing cooling joints. Vesicular zones along the margins and the centre suggest several pulses of melt injection.

Continue on the TF 28 through the villages of Charco del Pino and Granadilla. The uppermost part of the Cañadas 'Series', the Bandas del Sur Group of Brown *et al.* (2003), consists of **pyroclastic fall deposit**s (e.g. the 'Granadilla **pumice**' of Booth, 1973) and a number of major **ignimbrites**, all of which are products of a series of **plinian** eruptions from the Cañadas caldera.

Stop 4.2 (18.3 km; km post 72): Granadilla pumice fall deposit and ignimbrite in a small quarry west of La Cantera schoolhouse*** ^ See Update 12 on p.109.

Park outside the school yard, identified by two basketball posts. Walk back 100m along the road and take a track leading to the right. Examine the rock face on the

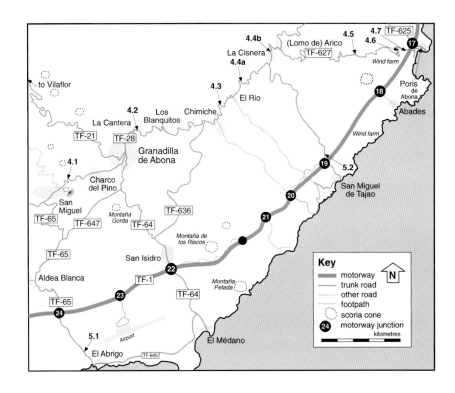

Figure 11. Sketch map showing the itinerary for Day 4 - Bandas del Sur.

Box 1: Types of pyroclastic deposit associated with plinian eruptions

How pyroclastic deposits are formed

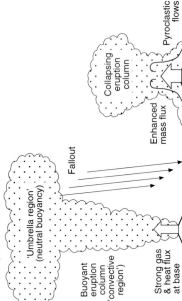

Buoyant column stage

Fallout

'Umbrella region' (neutral buoyancy)

Buoyant eruption column ('convective region')

Strong gas & heat flux at base

Volcano

Pyroclastic fountaining stage

Collapsing eruption column

Enhanced mass flux

Volcano

Pyroclastic flows

Pumice (or plinian) fall deposits testify to a vigorous eruption with a strong gas jet and a buoyant **eruption column** typically exceeding 15 km in height. This is favoured by a plentiful supply of volatile-rich magma and a high heat flux.

Pumice fall deposits accumulate in the early stages of a plinian eruption. Falling through the air produces a high degree of sorting, as fine ash is swept away by winds.

Ignimbrites (pumiceous **pyroclastic flow** deposits) are typically formed at the climax of a plinian eruption, when a high mass flux erupting through the vent generates a denser eruption column that entrains less air and cannot maintain buoyancy. Such a column 'collapses' to form pumiceous density currents (pyroclastic flows) that cascade down the flanks of the edifice. Cf. **block-and-ash flow**.

How to distinguish pyroclastic deposits

Pyroclastic fall deposits, whether derived from **plinian** or **strombolian** eruptions, consist of well sorted **lapilli** (of pumice or scoria respectively) with little ash. When deposited on undulating topography, they form beds of characteristically uniform thickness ('**mantle bedding** - see figure) that decreases with distance from the vent.

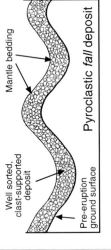

Mantle bedding

Well sorted, clast-supported deposit

Pre-eruption ground surface

Pyroclastic *fall* deposit

Ignimbrites and other pyroclastic flow deposits, on the other hand, are poorly sorted: lapilli are dispersed in an ashy matrix (**lapilli-tuff**). Being deposited from ground-hugging density currents, ignimbrites typically accumulate in valleys. An ignimbrite may be massive (Figure 13a), or may exhibit various forms of internal stratification (Figure 14a). See Box 2.

Concentrated in valleys

Poorly sorted, matrix-supported (ash-rich) deposit

Pyroclastic *flow* deposit

Ash

left that has a doorway excavated into its base. The pumice **lapilli** making up this deposit are angular and very well sorted (generally 0.5 - 3.0mm in diameter). In the context of pyroclastics, 'well sorted' means a clast-supported deposit with little fine ash between the pumice clasts (Figure 12) giving a freshly exposed surface a 'grainy' look. This deposit is typical of a pyroclastic fall blanket deposited by settling from the high buoyant **eruption column** (ash cloud) of a plinian eruption (Box 1); settling of pumice particles through the atmosphere allows the fine ash component to be winnowed away downwind. The white *Granadilla pumice* (Booth, 1973) at Stop 4.2 has sparse feldspar and occasional biotite phenocrysts, and chemical analysis shows it to be **phonolitic** in composition. The deposit also contains a small proportion of smaller light grey **lithic** fragments and scoria fragments, a distinctive feature of this pyroclastic formation.

Right at the top of the same face, on the right, can be seen a thin ashy pumice unit with low-angle cross-stratification, and above that a more massive bed rich in fine ash such that the pumice clasts are matrix-supported. These are products of the collapse of the plinian eruption column (Box 1), marking the end of its initial buoyant phase as the eruption column became denser because the vent had enlarged. Walk on to view the main quarry face 100 m further on, where the relationships are more easily examined.

The lower bed at the back of the pit is the pumice fall deposit just examined, of which about 5m is exposed. Such deposits blanket pre-existing topography (Box 1), and the undulating upper surface here parallels the terrain on which the pumice fall

Figure 12. Well sorted pumice fall deposit, Poris Formation (Stop 4.7).

Box 2: Ignimbrite structure and emplacement mechanisms

Features* to look for in a simple ignimbrite flow unit: the 'standard model'

Layer*	Characteristics
'Layer 2b'	Thickest layer consists of massive **lapilli-tuff**.
	Pumice clasts may show reverse grading.
	Lithic clasts commonly show normal grading.
'Layer 2a'	Finer-grained basal layer (≤1m) usually without lithics
'Layer 1'	Thin (cross-) stratified layer

after Sparks et al (1973)

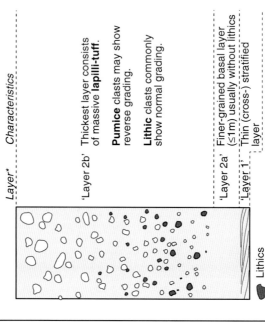

Lithics
Pumice
Ash

How are ignimbrites emplaced?

The 'standard model' for ignimbrite emplacement associated with plinian column collapse envisaged* an entire flow-unit being emplaced *en masse* by a single density-current pulse as it comes to rest. An idealized product of this model is shown in the figure left. It may be stratified in terms of texture and clast distribution, but it is compositionally homogeneous. Grading of lithics and pumices was considered to result from the *transport process*. Motion is made possible by a strong velocity gradient at the base of the flow, which generates the relatively fine-grained 'Layer 2a' by shearing.

Many ignimbrites fail to conform to the simple cross-section depicted in the figure. The 'standard model' cannot account for compositionally zoned ignimbrite flows, for internal stratification (*e.g.* **lithic**-rich horizons), or for the complex **welding** profiles seen in some ignimbrites; these internal variations point to changes with time during the *depositional* process. Branney and Kokelaar (1992, 2003) suggest an alternative emplacement model - now widely accepted - in which ignimbrites are deposited *progressively* from a *sustained*, pyroclastic 'density current'. In this *progressive aggradation* model, grading and welding profiles can be explained in terms of fluctuations in eruptive or depositional conditions as the eruption progresses. Finer-grained layers such as 'Layer 2a' - where it occurs - are attributed to fluctuation or 'unsteadiness' in the current velocity with time. Internal lithic-rich horizons (*e.g.* Figure 19) may be attributed to vent widening or erosion, or other causes of brittle strain (*e.g.* movement on caldera ring-fractures) taking place *during the course of a sustained eruption.*

Figure 13a The Granadilla ignimbrite north of Chimiche (Stop 4.3).
The view includes three massive layers of ignimbrite (boundaries arrowed).

Figure 13b. Detail of the fine laminated ash bed between lower two ignimbrite layers in Figure 13a.

Day 4. Cañadas succession in the 'Bandas del Sur' area

deposit was laid down. The stratified unit above is less clearly picked out by erosion here. Filling the depression in the underlying fall unit is about 6m of the ash-rich unit, known as the *Granadilla ignimbrite*, an **unwelded** pumiceous pyroclastic flow deposit, petrographically identical to the fall deposit and carrying the same pale grey lithic clasts. At the base is a 20cm layer of finer pumiceous ash (the so-called '2a layer' - see Box 2) above which the main body of the ignimbrite is texturally homogeneous, except for layers richer in larger lithic clasts. These lithic-rich bands suggest the ignimbrite was deposited progressively rather than as a single mass (Box 2); the lithics may relate to explosions that enlarged the vent during the course of the eruption or to episodes of caldera subsidence.

Box 1 shows how fall and flow deposits reflect different stages of plinian eruption. Most plinian-derived formations in the Bandas del Sur begin, like the Granadilla Formation (Table 2), with a pumice fall bed (sometimes several) which is overlain by one or more ignimbrite flow units. This common relationship suggests that the fall and ignimbrite components represent different phases in the evolution of a single plinian eruption (lasting from a few hours to a day or two). In support of this assertion we may note that no soil or weathered profile is seen between these units. Brown *et al.* (2003) obtained an Ar-Ar age for the Grandilla pumice fall deposit of 600 ± 9 ka.

The topography of these southeastern slopes seems to be defined principally by elongated phonolite lava flows mantled by Granadilla and later plinian pumice fall deposits (Table 2). The depressions between these flows have channelled **pyroclastic flows**. Other outstanding exposures of the Granadilla pumice can be seen by detouring southeast and driving along the secondary road from just north of San Isidro to Chimiche (TF-636).

A roadcut through one of these phonolite ribs (at 20.4km; *beware oncoming traffic*) exposes an excellent stratigraphic sequence of lava overlain by fall layers and various massive and stratified ignimbrites, with weathered horizons and unconformities indicating substantial intervals between several eruptive episodes. The roadcut provides a useful exercise in the logging and stratigraphic interpretation of a pyroclastic succession. **Accretionary lapilli** can be seen in an exposure 50m west of the roadcut.

Continue along the TF-28 across the Chimiche-Las Vegas road to stop 4.3 at 24.0km.

Locality 4.3 (24.0km): Granadilla pumice and ignimbrite in road-side quarry due north of Chimiche ***

After a sharp right bend where three doorways have been excavated from thick white Granadilla pumice fall deposit, the road leads past an imposing light beige quarry face in a 15m-thick unit of massive lapilli tuff (Figure 13), resting on a thick bed of plinian airfall pumice. This is one of the thicker parts of the Granadilla

Figure 14a (above) Moderately welded facies of the Arico ignimbrite in the Barranco del Azucar (Stop 4.4a), showing the boundary betwen the beige-brown and grey zones (see Figure 15).
Figure 14b (below) Unwelded facies of the Arico ignimbrite near Poris (Stop 4.6) showing abundant pumice lapilli and obsidian clasts. Note the brown-rimmed slightly inflated obsidian clast near the top.

ignimbrite (mapped by Araña & Coello, 1989 as the 'Chimiche ignimbrite').

The ignimbrite here is not **welded**, but its ashy matrix is slightly indurated (making it popular as a building stone hereabouts) and the pumice clasts have been altered and preferentially weathered out, making the rock appear at first glance coarsely vesicular. The base of the ignimbrite unit is most easily seen on the south side of the road, on the face of a small crag beneath a tree; note the thin, relatively fine-grained basal layer (*cf.* 'Layer 2a' in Box 2), resting directly on better-sorted pumice fall material beneath. The lower two massive layers of the ignimbrite are separated by a 5-10cm-thick laminated ash layer clearly seen in the main quarry face on the north side of the road (Figure 13b). Traditional thinking would describe this as a **pyroclastic surge** deposit, the product of a distinct, dilute, turbulent density current, emplaced during the hiatus between two successive ignimbrite flow units. In the progressive aggradation hypothesis of Branney and Kokelaar (2003) outlined in Box 2, however, the entire succession in this quarry could be seen as the product of a single sustained density current, the boundaries between the massive layers - including the laminated ash layer - representing no more than brief fluctuations in the properties (velocity, concentration, etc.) of an otherwise steady current.

The Granadilla ignimbrite seen in this quarry includes a third, more lithic-rich (but less cemented) ignimbrite layer at the top of the cliff. Tracing the succession SE-wards to the end of the quarry, it becomes clear that the lower two massive beds were separated in time by another ignimbrite layer that wedges out at the NW end of the quarry. These relationships illustrate the lateral variability of pyroclastic flows, and the capacity of pyroclastic density currents to erode as well as deposit (*cf.* Stop 5.2).

As at stop 4.2, the probability that both the pumice fall unit beneath (which lacks a weathered top) and the four ignimbrite layers above (together constituting the Granadilla Formation - Table 2) represent successive phases of the same plinian eruption can be discussed, as can the possible relationship to collapse of the Cañadas caldera. The Grandilla Formation is one of the thickest (locally exceeding 30m) and most widespread (> 500km^2) pyroclastic units in the Bandas del Sur succession. Bryan *et al.* (2000) provide minimum estimates (from proximal data only) of the total erupted volumes of the Granadilla pumice fall and ignimbrite of 5.1 and 5km^3 respectively; given the uncertainties in making such estimates (e.g. they do not include distal and offshore deposits), the true volumes erupted are likely to be considerably greater. Bryan *et al.* (2000) further propose that eruption occurred from two separate vents close to the southern margin of the Cañadas caldera, and the welded fallout deposits in the vicinity of Guajara peak (Excursion 7.1) are considered to be the near-vent facies of the same fallout blanket. Eruption column heights at various stages through the eruption are estimated to have been in the range 15-30km.

The Granadilla eruption marked the end of a period of intense pyroclastic activity between 670 and 600 ka (Table 2) - beginning with the eruption of the

Day 4. Cañadas succession in the 'Bandas del Sur' area

Arico ignimbrite seen at Stop 4.4 - and it was followed by a prolonged 300 ka pause in large-scale ignimbrite-forming eruptions, although the Aldea Blanca pumice-fall beds (Brown *et al.*, 2003), seen mantling the scoria beds at km 2.7 earlier in the day, were erupted during this period (Table 2).

Continue through El Rio as far as the Barranco del Azucar. Parking is available for 1-2 cars on the right just before TF-28 km post 64. However, there may be advantage in pulling off earlier into a disused length of old road on the right-hand side (SW side of barranco) as the road swings left down towards the bridge. Walk up the main road east of the bridge to the base of the Arico ignimbrite in the NE road cutting.

Stop 4.4 (26.2km): Welded Arico ignimbrite (localities 4.4a and 4.4b) ***

The Arico ignimbrite is a **peralkaline** phonolitic pyroclastic flow deposit containing pumice, black feldspar-phyric obsidian clasts and various lithic clasts. It was first recognised in barrancos in the neighbourhood of Arico, but occurs widely across the Bandas del Sur. As the only welded ignimbrite found in the Bandas del Sur, it provides a distinctive marker horizon (Bryan *et al.* 1998) in spite of showing marked lateral and longitudinal variation. In the Barranco del Azucar it consists of several distinct zones differentiated primarily by colour and degree of welding (Alonso *et al.* 1988; Bryan *et al.* 1998).

Stop 4.4a (26.2km by km post 64): Arico ignimbrite in the Barranco del Azucar ***

A 7m section of the Arico ignimbrite, resting on the weathered top of an older pumice fall unit (at least 3m thick), is seen to the left of the road as it traverses the northeast side of the barranco toward Arico, east of the bridge. The ignimbrite consists of several distinct zones, encountered in turn as one walks up the road cut, as summarized in Figure 15. The basal layer consists of a pale unwelded pumiceous lapilli-tuff containing sparse blocks (some quite large) of obsidian. This passes up quite sharply into a brown welded variant containing more obsidian, and this is followed, again quite sharply, by a 2m zone of variably welded grey lapilli-tuff (Figure 14a). This grades up into a pinky-brown welded layer almost devoid of obsidian that marks the top of the ignimbrite. It is overlain by dark lithic breccias, in one of which the dark clasts are strongly size-graded. The series of outcrops is capped by a dark, well jointed **sodalite**-bearing **mugearite** lava exposed by the road further up.

The constitution of the Arico ignimbrite here is perplexing. The abundance of obsidian clasts, which appear to be juvenile, is reminiscent of a **block and ash flow** or **nuée ardente** deposit but the intensity of welding and the lateral extent of the ignimbrite (Brown *et al.* 2003) argue against this interpretation. The origin and emplacement of the Arico ignimbrite will be discussed when other outcrops have

Day 4. Cañadas succession in the 'Bandas del Sur' area

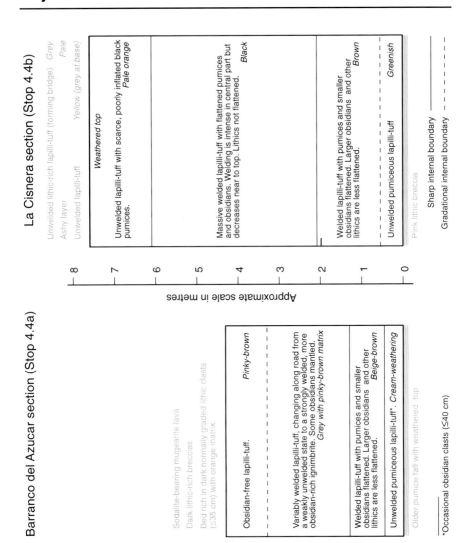

Figure 15. *Field logs through the Arico ignimbrite in the Barranco del Azucar and in la Cisnera village. Units shown in grey are not part of the Arico Formation.*

been visited.

Continue into the village of La Cisnera. Drive through until a point where the main road has been tunnelled through the ignimbrite (leaving behind a fragile-looking bridge capped by a wall), and park in the first side-turn on the right (shady parking).

Stop 4.4b (30.2km): Arico ignimbrite at bridge over road in La Cisnera ***

This is a thicker section of the Arico ignimbrite, exposed where the road has been cut through it. The uppermost preserved part of the Arico ignimbrite sheet can be seen underneath the bridge, and the base can be seen by walking onward down the road (*attention to traffic on blind bends here*). All parts of the ignimbrite here contain obsidian clasts; the main zones again differ in colour and degree of welding (Figure 15).

The lowest part of the ignimbrite, as at Stop 4.4a, consists of unwelded greenish, relatively pumiceous massive lapilli-tuff which grades up into brown-weathering welded ignimbrite (more correctly described as eutaxitic lapilli-tuff) containing flattened pumice and obsidian fiamme, together with non-flattened larger obsidian and lithic clasts. The brown layer shows a fairly sharp upward transition (over about 1cm) into 4m of black, massive, intensely welded lapilli-tuff that makes up the bulk of the road-cut up to the bridge, becoming less welded toward the top. Above there is a sharp transition to a pale orange unwelded lapilli tuff with poorly inflated dark clasts. It has what appears to be a weathered top and probably marks the top of the Arico Formation here. Three overlying ignimbrite layers can be seen at the bridge but they contain no obsidian.

Walking further down the road, one passes a ridge of basement (here an angular breccia) before re-entering the ignimbrite (near a short length of aqueduct), though the zonation is less clear here. Beyond a stone retaining wall, one can see that the ignimbrite (the 70cm thick unwelded basal layer) is underlain by a thin (a few cm) pumice fall bed. This fall layer is part of the same plinian eruption, and in other places is much thicker (Brown *et al*, 2003), but erosion by the ensuing pyroclastic flow has removed most of it here, and all of it at Stop 4.4a (where the underlying pumice fall bed had a weathered top so was clearly older). The pumice fall bed here rests on an older ignimbrite, probably of the Eras Formation (Table 2).

Continue to Arico (shown on some maps as 'Lomo De Arico', as distinct from Arico Viejo further on) and turn right towards Poris de Abona (TF-627).

Locality 4.5 (37.1km; between km posts 5 & 4): 'Wavy Deposit' beside the Arico-Poris road **

A distinctive bed informally known as the 'wavy deposit' (Martí *et al*. 1995; Bryan *et al*. 1998) is exposed in roadside cuttings (S side of road) but can be seen without disturbance from traffic in the banks of a minor road on the left; take care in parking not to obstruct the turn.

This intriguing stratified ash deposit (Figure 16) found in the Poris-Arico area

Figure 16. Hummock and lamination in bedded ash of the 'wavy deposit' overlain by plinian pumice fall layer (La Caleta Formation) beside the Arico-Poris road (TF-627) at Stop 4.5.

boasts almost as many explanations as outcrops! It forms the lowest part of the initial pumice fall deposit of the 221 ka La Caleta Formation of Brown *et al* (2003), and can be divided here into a lower crudely bedded lapilli-grade pumice unit around 12 cm thick ('layer A'), overlain by a white, finely laminated ashy layer of similar thickness ('layer B'). These layers are overlain by a well sorted pumice fall bed 2-3m thick, followed by the La Caleta ignmibrite (not obvious in the road-side exposures).

The main interest lies in the superficially dune-like forms in layer A which are draped by an unbroken bed of uniform thickness of layer B. Cavities are occasionally seen in these mounds. In 3D they are not dunes, as they have no traceable linear crests: the mounds are in fact **periclinal** in form. Martí *et al.* (1995) proposed a **base surge** (or **phreatomagmatic**) origin for the mounds, in which the ashy layer B represents a wetter second surge whose momentum and tractive capacity dragged the unconsolidated lower 'dry surge' layer A into crests shortly after deposition. A base-surge mechanism is hard to reconcile with the periclinal form of the mounds and the lack of any cross-stratification. Bryan *et al.* (1998) tentatively interpreted the mounds as water-escape structures, which fits their periclinal form but is at odds with the continuity of crude bedding through some of them. Brown *et al.* (2003) attribute the mounds to blanketing by layer A of small *Euphorbia* shrubs (since collapsed and rotted away); this explains the occasional cavities and plant remains and the spacing of the mounds (similar to the present-day spacing of spurge bushes on these hillsides), but it is not immediately clear why layer A thickens in the mounds.

Day 4. Cañadas succession in the 'Bandas del Sur' area

The La Caleta Formation here overlies a 1m lithic-rich ignimbrite unit of the Poris Formation (the Upper Grey Ignimbrite of Bryan *et al.* 1998) resting on a pumice fall deposit. Note the concentration of lithics near the base of the ignimbrite and the internal bedding picked out by coarser pumices in the centre.

Locality 4.6 (40.0km): Unwelded Arico ignimbrite **

After km post 2, the road executes three sharp left-right descending bends. After the second leftward bend but before the third (at 40.0km), unwelded Arico ignimbrite can be seen on the left of the road as it swings to the right; there is room for one car to pull off on the right before the rightward bend. The roadside outcrop begins with a brown-weathering calcreted overhang, is interrupted by a channeled debris deposit, and resumes as far as the third leftward bend. Here the ignimbrite contains relatively unflattened obsidian clasts and a higher proportion of pumice clasts which also show no flattening. A few pumices have dark poorly inflated interiors that look transitional to obsidian (Figure 14b), suggesting that the obsidian clasts have a juvenile origin and are not accidental inclusions (Brown *et al.* 2003). This exposure is more typical of the Arico ignimbrite as a whole than are the outcrops near La Cisnera.

Stop 4.7 (41.2 km): Accretionary lapilli at Poris quarry *

Just before the bridge under the Autopista above Poris de Abona, turn right into an open quarried area on the south side of the road. Examine the roadside quarry face NW of some fallen blocks. This quarry is the type locality of the distinctive creamy-white Poris Formation which, as redefined by Brown *et al.* (2003), embraces a series of phonolitic plinian fall deposits, ignimbrites, some containing lithic breccias, and volcaniclastic sediments that are considered to record a single sustained explosive eruption at 275 ka (Table 2). The object of interest at this stop is the **accretionary lapilli** that occur in ash beds above a basal pumice fall deposit (Figure 12). The lapilli range up to 5cm in diameter and when seen in cross-section show sharply bounded concentric internal laminations. The accretionary lapilli-bearing facies of the Poris Formation occurs quite widely in the NE Bandas del Sur and may be as much as 1m thick in places. It has been taken to indicate a phreatomagmatic element in the Poris eruption (as accretionary lapilli indicate a moist ash cloud), or could be the result of steam generation where hot pyroclastic flows entered the sea, except for the fact that the accretionary lapilli bed underlies (i.e. predates) the associated Poris ignimbrite at this locality.

Access to the autopista is via the village of Poris de Abona: drive through the tunnel, turn left at the T-junction, then follow the road round until it takes you up to the motorway intersection. To visit Stop 4.8 (not shown in Figure 11), drive N on the autopista to the next exit (Exit 16, Las Eras), cross over the motorway bridge and pull off on the right as the road bends rightwards and descends toward a road junction and the southbound side of the motorway.

Day 4.Cañadas succession in the 'Bandas del Sur' area

Stop 4.8 (Autopista exit 16 - Las Eras): Unwelded Arico ignimbrite ***

The roadcut on the left of the access road consists of unwelded Arico ignimbrite resting on a palaeosol formed on an earlier pumice fall deposit. As figured by Brown *et al.* (2003, fig. 6b), the Arico ignimbrite here has eroded gullies in the underlying palaeosol, and has removed its own pumice fallout deposit as well as parts of two older pumice-fall layers. In addition to the abundant dark lithic clasts here that define a diffuse bedding at the base of the lower massive division, there is also a lot of paler pumice that shows the inverse grading seen in many simple ignimbrites (Box 2); shiny dense obsidian is however entirely absent – yet another variant of this heterogeneous unit. The ignimbrite is overlain here by the 289 ka Fasnia Formation pumice fall deposit, the boundary between representing a gap of nearly 400 ka (Table 2).

Having gained at Stops 4.7 and 4.8 a more representative impression of the Arico ignimbrite, one is better able to assesss its origins. Recent mapping by Brown *et al.* (2003), shows that the Arico ignimbrite sheet is far more extensive than previouly supposed (being traceable from El Médano in the SW to Las Eras in the NE). Also, over most of its outcrop (c.f. Stop 4.6), it occurs as a vertically zoned pumice-rich ignimbrite, welded at some locations (as at Stop 4.4) but not at others. The marked abundance of obsidian seen around La Cisnera is atypical and at some (distal) outcrops (e.g. Las Eras) obsidian is completely absent. Like the other ignimbrite sheets in the Bandas del Sur, the Arico Formation seems to be the product of plinian column collapse producing pumiceous pyroclastic flows (Box 1). The occurrence of obsidian suggests that chilled, relatively degassed magma may have blocked the vent or formed a dome over it (Brown *et al.* 2003), and thereby became incorporated in the pyroclastic flows when the explosive eruption broke through. The ability of obsidian clasts to flatten is taken as a sign of a still-hot juvenile origin, rather than being cold accidental clasts. The Arico ignimbrite is now recognized to be much too extensive across the Bandas del Sur to have been formed as a **block-and-ash flow** as proposed by Alonso *et al.* (1988); such flows usually have a volume less than 1 km^3. The abundance of non-juvenile lithic clasts may relate to a caldera collapse event during the course of the eruption.

No quantitative estimate of the total volume of the Arico ignimbrite has been published but, in the light of their re-interpretation of its distribution, Brown *et al.* (2003) consider it to be of a similar order of magnitude to the other major explosive eruptions in the Bandas del Sur, and postulate that the ignimbrite's distribution indicates that the pyroclastic currents may have surmounted the S and E walls of the caldera in several places.

Day 5. The Cañadas succession (concluding) and the Cordillera Dorsal

A superb concluding overview of the Cañadas pyroclastic succession can be obtained by visiting the worked-out Tajao quarry, whose S-facing cliff is magnificently illuminated by morning sunshine. Having reviewed the closing stages of the construction of the Cañadas volcano, the excursion moves on to examine the voluminous outpourings of basalt that were taking place at the same time further to the northeast, forming the prominent NE-SW spine known as the Cordillera Dorsal. These eruptions began around 0.9 Ma ago and have continued to historic times. The landslide scars that have cut into the Cordillera Dorsal record episodes of sector collapse that testify to the inherent instability of oceanic island volcanoes.

Locality 5.1: Abrigo ignimbrite**

The day begins by visiting the youngest ignimbrite of the Bandar del Sur Group, the 169 ka Abrigo ignimbrite (Table 2). Take exit 24 from the Autopista del Sur signed to San Miguel, Los Abrigos and Las Galletas (the same exit as for the start of Day 4). This time,

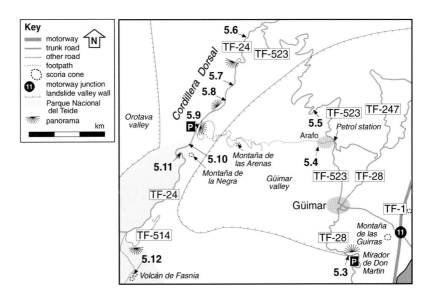

Figure 17. Sketch map for Day 5. NB the locations for stops 5.1 and 5.2 are shown in Figure 11.

Day 5. Cañadas succession and the Cordillera Dorsal

head SE down the TF-621 toward El Abrigo. Continue to the first turning in El Abrigo (also known as Los Abrigos), turn the car round and drive 250m back toward the motorway. The ignimbrite is exposed on the right in a narrow road cutting at the intersection with a track heading off to the NE (*busy main road - take care with passing traffic*).

The lower part of the ignimbrite is relatively lithic-poor and shows clear reverse grading of pumice clasts; the upper part is spectacularly lithic-rich, containing abundant clasts of basaltic scoria, syenite and microsyenite. The upper part of this ignimbrite also contains streaky dark-green pumices that are particularly evident at the top of the exposure. Such banded pumices are found in the upper parts of a number of Bandas del Sur ignimbrites, and also in the Diego Hernandez Formation of the caldera wall (Martí *et al.*, 1995). Discussion here may centre on:

- the significance of the high lithic content in the upper part of the Abrigo ignimbrite;
- what the compound structure of this ignimbrite says about its emplacement;
- the possibility of magma mixing in the formation of the heterogenous pumice lapilli;
- whether injection of fresh primitive magma (one factor in magma mixing) may have triggered some of the large ignimbrite-forming eruptions represented in the Bandas del Sur.

Rejoin the Autopista and exit at junction 19 signed to 'PIRS Tajao' and San Miguel de Tajao. Turn left at the end of the exit lane, cross the motorway and take the first turn on the right signed to La Cisnera. Pull off on the right beside a W-facing quarried face on the right beneath an electricity pylon; more parking is available at the far end of this face.

Locality 5.2: Tajao quarry ***

The S- and W-facing cliffs on the east side of the road provide excellent exposures of most of the Bandas del Sur pyroclastic succession (though the Eras and Arico Formations are below the level of exposure here). The sunlit S-facing cliff provides a good overview (Figure 18) from which the relative stratigraphic positions of the Granadilla Formation (*cf*. Stops 4.2, 4.3), the Poris Formation (Stop 4.7), the La Caleta Formation (Stop 4.5) and the Abrigo Formation (Stop 5.1) can be seen for the first time. One is immediately struck by the lack of planar boundaries, most of the units exhibiting considerable variation in thickness from one side of the face to the other, with some being pinched out entirely. This is partly because pyroclastic flows tend to fill pre-existing topographic depressions produced by subaerial erosion, but also reflects the intrinsic erosive power of the ignimbrites themselves during their emplacement. The Abades and Granadilla formations have been correlated with the Guajara Formation in the caldera wall (Table 2) while those above correlate with the Diego Hernandez Formation.

Some of the units seen in the S face can be examined close-up (helmet

Day 5. Cañadas succession and the Cordillera Dorsal

Figure 18. Annotated view of the Bandas del Sur pyroclastic succession exposed in the south-facing cliff of Tajao quarry (Stop 5.2) The height of the face is about 15 metres. The pale layer above the La Caleta pumice fall bed was identified by Martí et al. (1995) but is now believed to be the Abrigo ignimbrite (M. Branney, pers. comm.): note the yellowish soil capping the La Caleta pumice fall which implies erosion and a time gap bfore the overlying ignimbrite was emplaced.

recommended) in roadside section (Figure 19). At the foot of the face near the SW corner, the brownish Abades ignimbrite (more extensively exposed in the east-facing cliff set back on the other side of the road) contains distinctive black pumices as well as white, testifying to magma mixing during the course of eruption. It has a weathered top indicating a break in explosive activity. Above it lies the Granadilla pumice fall deposit with its characteristic small pale-grey lithics (*cf.* Stop 4.2), overlain at the north and south ends by a distinctive 'holey' ignimbrite (*cf.* Stop 4.3) A second palaeosol at the top of the ignimbrite marks another break in explosive activity; its continuity along the face suggests that the Granadillo ignimbrite had been partially removed by subaerial erosion before the emplacement of the overlying formation. The Fasnia Formation is represented in this face alone by a lens of lithic-rich ignimbrite (the 'Lower Grey Lithic Ignimbrite' of Bryan *et al.* 1998) that is pinched out in both directions by the overlying Poris ignimbrites, which include a second highly lithic unit (the 'Upper Grey Lithic Ignimbrite' of Bryan *et al.* 1998 c.f. Stop 4.5). The La Caleta Formation here consists solely of a 0.5m of pumice fall deposit, at the base of which is a finely laminated ash layer, the lateral equivalent of the 'wavy deposit' (Stop 4.5). The La Caleta ignimbrite appears to have been

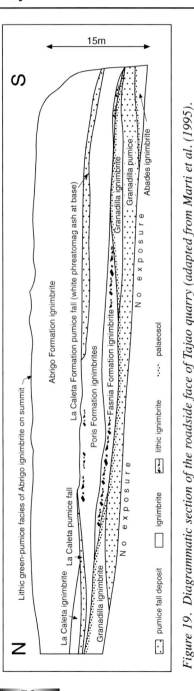

Figure 19. Diagrammatic section of the roadside face of Tajao quarry (adapted from Marti et al. (1995).

completely eroded away here (see Figure 18): the ignimbrite layers above the pumice fall appear to be those of the Abrigo ignimbrite (*cf.* Stop 5.1), which on this face has eroded away the soil capping the pumice fall in Figure 18. The lithic and green-streaky pumice facies is not visible from the road but can be examined by climbing a track up to the summit, the first right turn at the north end of the face.

Points to ponder:
• why are some ignimbrite units here rich in lithics, and others not? Might lithic content be a record of major tectonic disturbance during eruption (e.g. caldera subsidence)?
• if pumice fall deposits generally blanket the topography upon which they are deposited(Box 1), why are they mostly lensoid here?
• List the distinctive features that would enable positive identification at another locality, of each of the main formations represented here.

Rejoin the motorway and proceed to Exit 13, signed for El Tablado and El Escobonal. *Zero the trip recorder kilometres at this junction.*

Follow the TF-617 up to El Escobonal. The road zig-zags up an erosion surface that repeatedly intersects the junction between seaward-dipping Cordillera Dorsal basaltic flows, usually 1-2m thick with rubbly tops and bottoms, and Bandas de Sur pumiceous pyroclastics (pumice fall beds and ignimbrites) that rest unconformably on them. For example, a road cut 4.0km from the motorway exit (irrigation pipe above road) exposes the following succession:

5. Pumice-rich lapilli tuff, lower parts filling channels eroded in
   underlying beds;
4. Stratified ash layer a few cm thick;
3. Thin grey lithic-rich pumice lapilli tuff whose variable thickness up to
   35cm suggests channel filling or erosion;
2. Cream-coloured, coarsely stratified ash layer 20-30cm thick;
1. Weathered rubbly top of basaltic lava.

Here is another opportunity to debate whether beds 2-5 are products of discrete 'surge' and 'ignimbrite' density currents separated in time or whether they aggraded progressively from a single sustained pyroclastic current that fluctuated with time

At the T-junction at the top of the village of El Escobonal (6.4 km) turn right on the TF-28. This road winds repeatedly from basalts into overlying pyroclastics and back again. Note the widespread use of cut blocks of Granadilla ignimbrite for the construction of walls and occasional buildings hereabouts. Follow the road as far as the Mirador de Don Martin overlooking Güimar. Here the road bends sharply to the left and descends the dramatic southern side-wall of the Güimar valley (Figure 17). Parking is available just before the bend. *Small* groups may walk ~100m down the road (**NB** *traffic hazard – see p. 5*) to a point where a parapet overlooking the valley begins on the right; from here a fine panorama of the Güimar valley can be seen and discussed.

Stop 5.3 (14.6 km): Güimar[15] valley and Dorsal basalts from the Mirador de Don Martin***

The Cordillera Dorsal ridge is cut into by two prominent valleys (centred on and named after the towns of Güimar to the SE and La Orotava to the N) that are evidently the result of large-scale landslides (examples of **lateral** or **sector collapse**). The pronounced SW and NE side-walls of the Güimar valley and its headwall are clearly seen from this panorama. Investigations in deep water-supply tunnels show that the floor of the valley is underlain by more than 100m of debris avalanche deposit (Ancochea *et al.*1990), and a bathymetric high offshore suggests where the slipped material has come to rest (Teide Group, 1987). The lateral collapse must post-date the youngest lava in the landslide scarp (to which Ancochea *et al.* 1990 give a K-Ar age of 830 ka), and Brown *et al.* (2003) have dated the oldest-known post-collapse pyroclastic formation found in the valley (the Fasnia Formation, Table 2) by Ar-Ar at 289±6 ka; the collapse must have occurred between these two times but no more precise constraint is available. The Recent Montaña Grande cone and a few smaller

---

[15] Pronounced 'Gweemar'

Day 5. Cañadas succession and the Cordillera Dorsal

Figure 20. Succession of plinian fall deposit, basaltic scoria, and columnar-jointed basaltic lava flow at Stop 5.5.

cones have been constructed on the landslide apron directly below, discharging a lava flow across it. Beyond the town of Güimar the 1704/5 basalt lava flow from Montaña de las Arenas (stop 5.9) forms a positive feature running down the centre of the valley, sparsely vegetated with small pine trees (see Stop 5.4).

Small parties can walk down the road to examine a section through the 800m-thick sequence of Dorsal basalts and ankaramites in the valley wall; *great care should be taken to manage the constant traffic; these exposures are* **not** *safe for larger parties*. The sequence, superficially similar to OBS but with ages younger than 0.9 Ma, consists of basalts and ankaramites. Beyond the 29km post, the flows become thinner (30-50cm) and more vesicular. A 2.5m-thick, well jointed flow can be seen immediately after a steep track on the left.

Proceed through Güimar to Arafo. The signing in Güimar is non-existent! Once you have entered a small one-way system (18.7km), filter left at the first petrol station (50m), turn right at the main road (two-way road – right-filter at traffic light opposite the Oficina de Ventas), left at a rather inconspicuous orange sign to Pyramides de Güimar on the wall of the Caja Rural on the left (by CEPSA filling station), then right at a T-junction on to the main road to Arafo (TF-523).

Day 5. Cañadas succession and the Cordillera Dorsal

Stop 5.4 (21.6 km): Arafo cemetery / Campo de futbol *

A diversion may be made on the outskirts of Arafo (left turn) to the football pitch at the SW corner of the town, which is built between the levées of one lobe of the 1704/5 lava from the scoria cone of Montaña de las Arenas high above on the Dorsal flanks. The outcrop of the lava uphill can be picked out by the sparse cover of relatively young pine tree (*cf*. Stop 5.9).

On reaching a 5-way junction by a petrol station east of Arafo old town (22.4km, not allowing for diversion to the football stadium), continue across on the TF-523, following signs to El Teide. Continue up the winding, well made road that leads up the head-wall of the valley. Numerous road-cuts offer excellent exposures of later basalts coating the hillside, representing post-landslide eruptions from vents close to the Cordillera Dorsal. These basalts and the associated scoria beds are often interbedded with late Cañadas plinian pumice fall deposits, sometimes with alternations of beds only a few cm thick. No ignimbrites are found here, presumably because these northern locations did not lie directly down-slope from the plinian vents associated with the Cañadas caldera.

Stop 5.5 (26.7 km):   Basalt / pyroclastic exposure in the head-wall of the Güimar valley *

An typical exposure is found on the right hand side before a left-hand bend in the road (Figure 20). It shows a plinian fall deposit (white), overlain by a topography-mantling bed of basaltic scoria (with finely interbedded scoria and pumice at the base), which is overlain by a columnar-jointed basaltic lava with a rubbly base; flow-striations in the massive basalt indicate it was flowing approximately at right angles to the road.

The basalt sequences contain both simple and compound flows; some simple flows are remarkably thin. Scoria beds and dissected scoria cones are much in evidence in the upper part of the succession, interdigitated with basaltic and trachybasaltic flows and with further pale plinian airfall horizons. Toward the top of the road, where the ridge is cloaked with magnificent woods of Canary Pine (*Pinus canariensis*) and occasional Eucalyptus, outcrops of older Dorsal flows exhibit extensive weathering and it becomes difficult to distinguish between lavas and scoria banks.

Turn left on to the TF-24 road running up the crest of the Cordillera Dorsal (40.5 km). Stop at a small flat area on the right at 41.8km.

---

[16] *For visitors starting this traverse from a different direction, the second km figure refers to the distance from the TF-523/TF-24 intersection.*

Day 5. Cañadas succession and the Cordillera Dorsal

*Figure 21a. (above)
Spatter bank forming
part of a scoria/spatter
cone complex at Stop 5.8
beside the summit road
(TF-24) on the
Cordillera Dorsal.*

*Figure 21b. (below)
Spatter reinforcing the
interior of the 1705
Volcan de Fasnia cone
(Stop 5.12); size 7 boots
for scale.*

Day 5. Cañadas succession and the Cordillera Dorsal

Stop 5.6 (41.8 / 1.3km[16]): Panorama of the valley of La Orotava, Teide and La Palma **

The valley of La Orotava is the second of the two landslip-formed valleys carved in the side of the Cordillera Dorsal (*cf.*Stop 5.3). This valley is bounded by steep side-walls and headwall just as impressive as those defining the Güimar valley. The approximate age of this valley is bracketed by *(a)* the youngest K-Ar age on basalts in the valley wall (0.78 Ma) and *(b)* a K-Ar age of 0.56 Ma for a lava spilling over one of the scarps (Ancochea *et al.* 1990). Northeasterly trending dykes and sub-ordinate sills can be seen in the headwall of the valley and along the roadside exposures. The buttressing effect of the Cañadas and Anaga edifices - at each end of the Cordillera Dorsal - and its possible control of extension, dyke emplacement and slope failure can be discussed.

This stop provides the first clear view of Teide (3718m), with the pale shoulder of the Montaña Blanca volcano (2690m) in front. On a clear day the island of La Palma can be seen to the right. Similar views free of passing traffic can be obtained from the Mirador de las Cumbres, the turn-off for which is at 43.0 / 2.5km (detour not included in km data for succeeding stops). Continue along the road and stop stop on the left about 400m beyond the Fuente de Joco.

Stop 5.7 (43.9 / 3.4km): Near Fuente de Joco *

Look out for two radially jointed bodies of grey **trachybasalt** lava on the right of the road, 400m beyond the Fuente de Jaca. These rounded bodies are massive in the centre with increasing degrees of vesicularity toward the margins, particularly on the upper side where the load pressure would have been least. Radial jointing implies a cylindri-cal cooling surface perpendicular to the bank in which it is exposed, and these bodies appear to represent lava tubes or channels filled with lava that did not drain from the tube and cooled by losing heat to the brecciated carapace surrounding them.

Continue along the road and park on the right by TF-24 km post 28 (45.0km from El Escobonal junction, 4.5 km from T-junction). Walk back 90m.

Stop 5.8 (45.0 / 4.5km): Basaltic spatter bank and dissected composite scoria cones ***

On the SE side of the road a basaltic dyke can be seen feeding a spatter bank (Figure 21a), consisting of a towering pile of flattened basaltic clasts that have evidently landed in a ductile or semi-molten condition and welded on to those lower in the pile, typical of **hawaiian**-type basaltic lava fountaining and near-vent **strombolian** deposits (*cf.* Stop 5.12). Returning 30m toward the parking place, a series of columnar-jointed lavas can be seen banking against, and in some cases overflowing, crystal-rich scoria beds that are the remnants of a scoria cone; here again there is evidence of both strombolian (scoria) and hawaiian phases of activity. This

Figure 22a (above) Interbedded pumice and scoria fall beds (Stop 5.11).
Figure 22b (below) Close up showing low-angle cross-stratification. Large red
penknife (8.5 cm; left bottom corner) for scale.

Day 5. Cañadas succession and the Cordillera Dorsal

is an excellent location for sketching and analysing the sequence of eruptive events.

Note a richly pyroxene-phyric lava and pyroxene- and hornblende-rich tuffs a little further to the SW. All of these exposures are cut by a swarm of northeasterly-trending dykes, some of which show flow-direction indicators: in one exposure tube vesicles indicate near-horizontal magma flow.

Proceed to a tourist board labelled La Crucita at 47.3km and park on the right hand side of the road. Cross the road carefully to the display boards on the SE side.

Stop 5.9 (47.1 / 6.6km): La Crucita and 'Caldera de Pedro Gil': panorama of Montaña de las Arenas scoria cone, the Güimar valley and Gran Canaria ***

This stop provides an excellent retrospective of the Güimar valley below, defined by clear landslide scarps to south and north. From Stop 5.9 the black cone of Montaña de las Arenas (source of the 1704/5 flow seen at stop 5.4) can be seen nestling in the amphitheatre immediately below (known as 'Caldera de Pedro Gil' though not a caldera in the geological sense) and is easily visited by means of a dirt road. In clear weather, the main features of the neighbouring island of Gran Canaria (80km distant) can be seen from here.

On the NW side of the road, scoria beds have banked up against a pre-existing cliff formed in earlier plagioclase-phyric basalt lavas. Whether these are distal scoria deposits from Montaña de las Arenas or a neighbouring scoria cone is not clear from the dip of the bedding.

At 47.5 / 7.0km, the first fresh black scoria beds of the Montaña Negra basaltic centre are seen beside the road. This was a relatively long-lived centre of fairly recent caldera-rim strombolian activity (a precise age is not known). Turn off on the right of the road at 48.2 / 7.7 km.

Stop 5.10 (48.2 / 7.7km): Scoria beds from the Montaña Negra strombolian centre **

Exposures along the left hand side of the road provide evidence of the longevity of this centre:
- A little way back down the road can be seen an unconformity in which an erosion surface on earlier red scoria beds has been covered by later black scoria. A number of such unconformities can be seen between here and stop 5.11.
- 100m to SW, a dyke can be seen cutting young basaltic scoria. It is narrow at the base but broadens out upslope. This may have been a conduit supplying later strombolian eruptions.

Stop 5.11 (49.1km):   Road bends beneath Montaña de la Negra ***

NB. *You have now entered the Parque Nacional del Teide: from this point on, the collecting of any specimens (geological or botanical) is prohibited. Wardens patrol regularly to enforce this restriction.*

Day 5. Cañadas succession and the Cordillera Dorsal

Below Montaña Negra (2241m) the road zig-zags up through dramatic road-cuts (Figure 22) exposing interbedded plinian (white) phonolitic pumice fall deposits and **strombolian** (black **scoria**) deposits with minor interbeds of hydroclastic material (cross-bedded with unoccupied bomb sags and sparse cauliflower bombs).

The upper parts of the pumice layer (Figure 22b) display an upward transition from (a) moderately well sorted pumice lapilli (plinian fall deposit), into (b) stratified pumice lapilli-tuff, into (c) brownish laminated beds with a higher proportion of angular scoria lapilli and exhibiting low-angle cross-stratification. The stratified beds here may represent (b) deposition from an unsteady pyroclastic current derived from the plinian eruption, and (c) **base-surge** deposits from small **phreatomagmatic** explosions (steam-generating interactions between ascending basaltic magma and an aquifer within late-Cañadas pumiceous pyroclastics), but it is hard to eliminate the possibility of epiclastic reworking of pyroclastic material.

This interbedded scoria-pumice relationship, repeated in gullies below the road, correlates with the uppermost levels of the Diego Hernandez succession (Excursion 6.6B - see also Araña &Coello, 1989, p.220). It testifies to the contemporaneous existence below different sectors of central Tenerife of two separate, and radically different, magma plumbing systems:

(a) a very large, long-lived magma chamber (or system of chambers) directly beneath the caldera that had fractionated – at least in the upper parts – to form evolved phonolite magma, which fed the periodic large plinian eruptions whose pumiceous ejecta are seen at this stop, in the caldera wall and in the Bandas del Sur succession (Table 2). The magmatic cycles seen in the caldera wall (Martí *et al.* 1997) suggest that this magma fractionation process was repeated a number of times.

(b) a smaller-volume but on-going basaltic magma-supply system that provided more rapid transit through the crust (too quickly for magma to fractionate to more evolved compositions) and fed a succession of small strombolian eruptions. This plumbing system has supplied cones on the flanks of the caldera, but looking across towards Teide from this locality it is clear that a significant number of such cones have also formed near the northern margin of the caldera, and one – the **breached** cone of Montaña Mostaza – on its floor. The absence of such cones from most other parts of the caldera floor, however, suggests that the large magma chamber supplying the plinian eruptions – (a) above – has obstructed the access of basaltic magma to the surface here: basaltic magma entering such a body of low-density evolved magma would find itself trapped in the lower levels by virtue of its greater density, where it would in due course fractionate to add to the volume of more evolved magma in the chamber. It may be that injection of basic magma into the base of a larger, more evolved chamber could trigger a large-scale eruption from the latter, as appeared to happen at Pinatubo in 1991.

Continue to the Observatory turn on the left (54.8 km), proceed up this road for 500 m and pull off. Close to the eastern caldera rim, looking due S, can be seen a number of Recent scoria cones. Among them it is not difficult to identify the

Day 5. Cañadas succession and the Cordillera Dorsal

1704/5 cones of Volcán de Fasnia, built of fresh black basaltic scoria, that erupted in December 1704 and continued erupting until March 1705. (This volcano is marked as Montaña del Roquillo on the Kompass map.) Lava erupted from both cones and threatened the town of Fasnia in the Bandas del Sur directly below. These cones are aligned on a fissure that also passes through the Montaña de las Arenas seen at stop 5.9, from which the Arafo flow erupted during the same winter.

The Fasnia cones are easily visited by returning to the intersection of the observatory road with the TF-24, and walking down the dirt track on the left that leads towards the cones (30 minutes each way); note the pumice fall beds and lithic-rich ignimbrites overlying older scoria beds (*cf*. Stop 5.11) exposed in the road cut where the track zig-zags across a barranco.

Excursion 5.12 (55.8 km): Volcán de Fasnia cones (AD 1705 eruption) *** ^^

The Fasnia cones are topographically very fresh and well worth visiting[17] to see reddish spatter banks on the inside rims of the cones (Figure 21b; *cf*. Stop 5.8) and a large volcanic bomb (a metre in diameter) perched on the rim of one cone. The volcano consists of a series of pits aligned NE-SW, and scoria-covered lava fields extend to the SE from these pits. A black scoria fall blanket can be seen on the other (N) side of the track, partially covered by downwash from slopes to the north.

Return to the main road, turn left and descend to the La Orotava intersection ('El Portillo'), turning left again toward the Parque Nacional del Teide proper (TF-21). Cafés at the intersection itself and further up the TF-21 offer refreshment, maps and postcards. The Visitor Centre on the right-hand side a few hundred metres up the TF-21 (carpark in front of 4 doors set in a stone wall) is worth visiting for exhibits on all aspects of the natural history of the Park; leaflets, maps and helpful advice on access in the Park can be obtained here; be sure to pick up a copy of the official *Mappa del Parque Nacional del Teide* which shows the boundaries of the Parque and the authorized walking routes within it (and the numbers by which they are signed). There is also a botanical garden illustrating Las Cañadas flora that is well worth visiting. A bookstall (closed at weekends) sells books, maps and cards.

The direct route back to south coast resorts leads through the Las Cañadas caldera and offers a foretaste of the final four days, which will be spent within the National Park or on its borders. Proceed to the road intersection in the southwest corner, and take either the road signed to Vilaflor (TF-21) and then Arona (TF-51), or the faster road to Chio (TF-38) from where the southern resorts can be reached on the TF-82.

---

[17] A faded barely legible wooden sign asks you not to climb the cones, but it has been comprehensively disregarded. Visitors should keep to existing tracks up the cones in order to avoid causing further erosion.

Day 6. Las Cañadas caldera

Note - The final three days are spent mostly in the Parque Nacional del Teide (Figure 23). In order to protect a fragile desert ecosystem and prevent erosion, access to areas within the Park is carefully regulated by the Park authorities. *Collecting any rock or plant material is strictly forbidden in all parts of the Park.* It is important that geological visitors respect these restrictions.

Most of the Park is classified as a 'restricted use area' in which visitors are merely required to keep to established tracks. Certain parts of the caldera wall, the Teide crater and the Pico Viejo caldera floor, are however classed as 'reserve' areas that are closed to

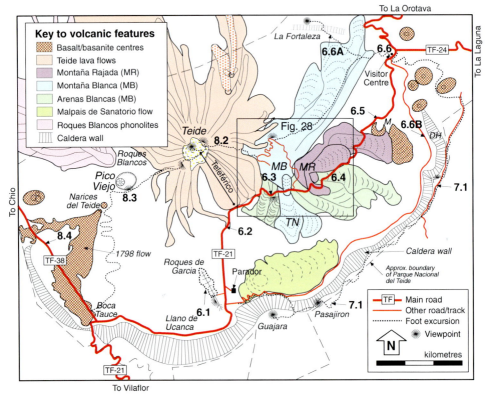

Figure 23. Sketch map showing stops in the Caldera de las Cañadas. The geology shown is greatly simplified. Abbreviations: DH Diego Hernandez sector of caldera wall, MB Montaña Blanca, MR Montaña Rajada, M Montaña Mostaza, TN El Tabonal Negro. The rectangle centred on MB indicates the area shown in more detail in Figure 28.

visitors, and *permission must be sought in advance* before attempting to visit such areas (notably the superb cliffs at Diego Hernandez seen from a distance on Excursion 6.6B). Enquiries regarding special access should be addressed in advance to:

Oficina del Parque Nacional del Teide
c/ Doctor Sixto Perera González, n° 25
38300 La Orotava Santa Cruz de Tenerife
Tenerife, Spain

Telephone	+34 922 92 23 71
Fax	+34 922 32 64 97
E-mail	pnteide@tenerife.es

One of the pleasantest routes into the Parque from the south and west of the island is the TF-38 ascending from Chio (Figure 23). Examples of drained lava tubes can be seen along the lower parts of this road (Figure 24); caution should be exercised if entering the largest of these (10.3 km from the Chio intersection, on the right opposite a track signed Posta Cueva de los Pajaros) as sections of roof look very insecure. The drive across the southern sector of the caldera (Llanos de Ucanca) toward stop 6.1 offers superb views of the lava flows that have cascaded down the southern slopes of Teide (Figure 25).

The day's stops begin at the Roques de Garcia carpark (stop 6.1). As the TF-21 road leaves the flat alluvial plain of Llanos de Ucanca and ascends leftward towards the Roques, note the spectacular pale turquoise-coloured altered rocks known as Los Azulejos, particularly on the right hand side of the road. These are located where one would expect to find the ring-fault system that has accommodated caldera subsidence, and the alteration testifies to the movement of hydrothermal fluids up the fracture system. The colour is not the result of copper mineralisation, the concentration Cu being less than 10 ppm (Araña & Coello, 1989, p.311-4). Petrographic and X-ray diffraction study shows that alteration of volcanic material has introduced zeolites, smectites and illite (Araña & Coello, 1989).

Turn left into the Roques de Garcia car- and coach-park. *Valuables should not be left in unattended vehicles as thefts are common.*

Excursion 6.1: Roques de Garcia *** ^^

This visit is best made early in the morning before tourist coaches arrive, or after 3 pm when most have departed. Note that the Roques are patrolled by Park officials, so visitors are advised to keep to the marked paths.

The Roques de Garcia pinnacles make up a spur or 'septum' of pre-caldera-fill rocks (belonging to the Lower Group of Martí *et al.* 1994) that divides the present caldera floor into two main segments (Figure 23), differing in elevation by about 70-100m, and this division has prompted the suggestion of two (or more - see Martí & Gudmundsson, 2000) separate caldera-forming events. The viewpoint (mirador)

Day 6. Las Cañadas caldera

Figure 24. Drained lava tube beside the TF-38 Chio to Boca Tauce road.

Figure 25. The Roques de Garcia and Pico del Teide viewed from the south across the Llano de Ucanca (Day 6). Note how the Roques have been swamped at their northern end by the accumulation of Teide lavas around them. The pronounced shoulder beneath the present summit cone of Teide marks the location of earlier nested summit craters.

overlooks the Llano de Ucanca, an alluvial basin trapped between young flow-fronts of **tephriphonolite** lava derived from Pico Viejo (Martí *et al.* 1995) and the southern caldera wall (see Figure 23 and lower picture on rear cover). At their northern end, the Roques have been overwhelmed by somewhat older lavas from the Teide-Pico Viejo complex. The northeastern part of the caldera has more varied fill, consisting of lava domes erupted from vents located on the caldera floor itself, lava and pyroclastic products from the Montaña Blanca centre, and most recently from Teide.

Despite its tourist popularity, the circular walk around the Roques (taking 1-2 hours) offers some excellent insights into the complexities of volcano instability. The dominant formation throughout the bulk of the pinnacles is a poorly sorted, matrix-supported polylithic breccia, best interpreted as a volcanic **debris avalanche** deposit representing an episode of gravitational instability in part of the Cañadas volcanic edifice. Avalanche deposits are a common feature of ocean islands and their offshore sedimentary aprons (including the Canary Islands themselves - see Watts & Masson, 1995; Cantagrel *et al.* 1999; Masson *et al.* 2002). Though the crude bedding generally dips in toward the present caldera, it is not clear whether the deposit represents local inward-directed collapse of an early caldera wall, or flank collapse of an external sector of the Cañadas volcano. Cantagrel *et al.* (1999) argued that this unit has characteristics of a landslide deposit, and regard it as the proximal facies of a very large debris avalanche deposit underlying the floor of the Icod valley running down the northwest slopes of the Cañadas edifice. Martí *et al.* (1995, p.94), however, note that drilling in the caldera floor to a depth of 500m has failed to intersect such 'landslide deposits', suggesting they may be less laterally extensive than envisaged by Cantagrel *et al.* (1999). Araña & Coello (1989, p.81) suggested that the Roques de Garcia avalanche deposit may have a **laharic** origin but the matrix is often insufficiently muddy to support this interpretation.

The breccia is seen first at the main mirador (where it is relatively finely bedded and locally contains puzzling tabular bodies – some with internal bedding – that may be rip-up clasts), and continues alongside the trail running northwards along the ENE margin of the pinnacles in coarser, more massive form as far as the first major gap in the pinnacles to the left of the path. In the intervening exposures, the breccia is cut by abundant irregular **cone sheets** (picked out by their oblique columnar jointing), striking initially at roughly 125° but swinging toward 090° the further north one goes. The dip of the cone sheets to the NE and N, together with the fact that such inward-dipping intrusions are characteristic of uplift rather than subsidence, suggests they could represent a period of resurgence (structural doming caused by a large body of buoyant - low density - magma beneath) of the northeastern caldera floor, after its initial collapse. Martí *et al.* (1995) suggest that the pre-caldera rocks of the Roques may themselves have been exhumed by this resurgence.

At the first prominent gap in the pinnacles can be seen beds of **accretionary**

Figure 26. Trachybasalt lava that has cascaded down a cliff between neighbour-ing Roques de Garcia pinnacles (Excursion 6.1). The left hand pinnacle is cut by cone-sheets and dykes. Note the dribble of trachybasalt lava poised at the extreme top-left. A minute figure on the skyline of the main flow and another in a white shirt in the cleft at the top left provide scale.

lapilli (*cf.* Stop 4.7) forming a lens within the breccia, and nearby an exposure of well bedded sandstones with wave ripples. The significance of the latter is unclear; one possibility is that the sediments were deposited on the floor of an early ephemeral caldera lake.

The major pinnacle to the north of this gap appears from its quasi-radial sub-horizontal columnar jointing to be a volcanic neck or plug, punching through the breccia. Such bodies are found in various places along the interior of the Cañadas caldera wall, where they seem to represent localised leakage of magma up an early ring fracture responsible for caldera subsidence. The presence of such bodies along the Roques gives support to the view (Araña & Coello, 1989; Martí *et al.* 1994) that the Roques de García constitute a screen of pre-caldera rocks that defines the boundary between two separate caldera structures formed at different times. At least some of the succeeding series of pinnacles probably represent necks too, though the abundance of dykes and cone sheets cutting them makes the identifica-tion less clear.

Some distance to the right of the trail lies the prominent flow front of a orange-weathering sparsely feldspar-phyric Teide phonolite lava with a very rubbly, pumiceous **a'a**-style surface. Between this flow and the path, as the trail climbs

Figure 27. Radiating subhorizontal columnar cooling joints on the western face of La Catedral (Excursion 6.1), an isolated volcanic neck exposed by erosion. Columnar joints form perpendicular to a cooling surface, which in this case approximated to an irregular vertical cylinder.

toward the northern termination of the Roques, lies an older, darker, richly porphyritic Teide lava, characterised by a smoother surface reminiscent of pahoehoe basalt lava, and a black glassy matrix. This earlier **trachybasalt** flow has formed an impressive cascade of pahoehoe-like lava flowing SW over a cliff between the two end pinnacles. Turning the corner in the path and descending a little way, one can see this cascade from the other side, and note another tongue of the same flow that froze on the brink in a neighbouring gap in the ridge without overflowing (Figure 26). The descending path follows the main flow for several hundred metres. Consider why the feldspar phenocrysts appear to lie selectively parallel to the surface of the flow. This flow appears to have been overrun by a younger more rubbly one, with randomly oriented feldspar phenocrysts, that forms a prominent flow-front facing the Llano de Ucanca.

The path passes to the left of a prominent free-standing pair of crags called La Catedral rising from the Llano de Ucanca, whose prominent radial jointing (Figure 27) identifies them as further volcanic necks. Climbing back toward the mirador up the linking spur from La Catedral, note the prominent near-vertical columnar jointing in the lithology that forms the small hill to the south-east (right) of the mirador. On close inspection, this unit has a flinty appearance with small white spherules that indicate **devitrification** of an originally glassy matrix. This unit, compositionally a trachyphonolite, was either a near-surface minor intrusion or a lava dome erupted on the surface. Its temporal relationship to caldera formation is unclear.

The next four stops lie beside the National Park road (TF-21) from the Roques de Garcia to El Portillo (the Visitor Centre). *The kilometre data for the rest of the day begin at the Roques carpark – reset your trip recorder here.*

Stop 6.2 (2.4 km): Frente de Avance, Colada del Teide *

This roadside sign marks where the road passes the flow front of an older, brown-weathered glassy phonolite lava that has descended from the southern flank of Teide (Figure 23). This flow is significantly older than the black flows that the road crosses at Stop 6.3.

Stop 6.3 (5.2km): Mirador 'El Tabonal Negro' below La Herreria ***

The viewpoint is situated where the road crosses a complex of flows that have issued from the Montaña Blanca vent (Figure 28a). These flows have cascaded down the relatively steep southern flanks of Montaña Blanca (the rounded mass above the road) between well developed levées that can be examined by walking 200-300m east along the road; to avoid traffic danger, it is possible to scale a low wall, but take particular care descending.

Below the road where the the largest lava lobe meets the lower gradient of the

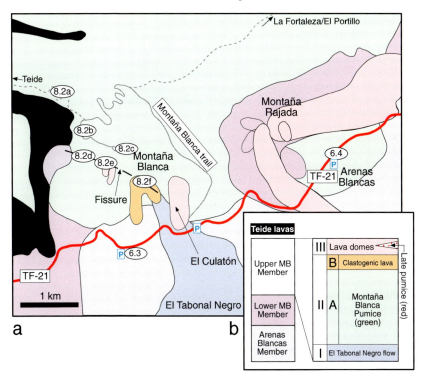

*Figure 28a. Geological map of the Montaña Blanca complex (after Martí et al. 1995 fig. 2). Figures in ellipses are locality numbers (Days 6 and 8). **P** = parking.*
Figure 28b. The stratigraphy of the Montaña Blanca complex, simplified after Ablay et al. (1995).

caldera floor, it spreads laterally forming the ridged lava platform of El Tabonal Negro; the direction of 'flow' can be deduced from the curvature of the arcuate surface ridges, which represent internal **ramping** of the viscous/glassy lava. The front of the flow has a classic frontal apron of flow breccia. This lava forms the lowest unit of the Upper Montaña Blanca Member of Ablay *et al.* (1995) - see Figure 28.

To the west, above the road, note the empty levées of young glassy phonolite flows that have flowed ESE from the summit region of Teide and been diverted through almost 90° to the SSW by the mass of Montaña Blanca in their path (see front cover and Figure 31). Teide flows are much more strongly feldspar-phyric than the obsidian from Montaña Blanca and Rajada.

Proceed along the road to a wide, undulating area with a thick carpet of pumice lapilli signed as Arenas Blancas, where there is plenty of space to pull off the road.

Day 6. Las Cañadas caldera

Stop 6.4 (7.9km): Arenas Blancas (= white sands) ***

Above the road are two lobes of the Montaña Rajada dome-flow (Figure 28a). Spilling down the side of the older right-hand one is a **pahoehoe**-like **coulée** of lava with draped surface corrugations, a form typical of Montaña Rajada (*cf*. Figure 36). The draping effect arises because the ductile glassy skin becomes pinned at the slow-moving margins of the flow, while the centre continues to move forward owing to the frictional drag of still-flowing lava beneath it. Such coulées indicate that the dome has grown by leakage of lava from vents near to its summit, the style of construction of an **exogenous** lava dome.

The stratigraphy of the Montaña Blanca (MB) volcano complex has been divided into three members by Ablay *et al.* (1995), shown in slightly simplified form in Figure 28b. The El Tabonal Negro lava flow (seen from Stop 6.3) is the basal component of the uppermost Upper Montaña Blanca Member, followed by the Montaña Blanca Pumice. Radiocarbon dating of charcoal from the MB Pumice shows that this member is the product of an eruption about 2000 years ago. The character of that eruption can be inferred from its pyroclastic products carpeting the ground to the south of the road.

The pumice lapilli beds here rest on an older Montaña Blanca phonolite flow of the Arenas Blancas Member . In several places south of the road it is possible to see that two pumice horizons are present: an older greenish white one (the Montaña Blanca Pumice = unit IIA in Figure 28b), overlain by a reddish, less inflated pumice (belonging to unit III). Differences in clast size, rounding and lithic content can be noted. The older pumice appears to be absent from both Rajada coulées, and the latter is very thin on the younger (left hand) Rajada lobe, leading to an inferred local stratigraphic sequence: (a) Montaña Blanca lava; (b) Montaña Blanca (green) Pumice eruption; (c) Montaña Rajada older lava lobe; (d) later red pumice eruption; (e) younger Rajada coulées. Similar relationships can be seen on top of Montaña Rajada from Excursion 8.2.

The greenish MB Pumice is quite widely spread across the NE sector of the caldera (*e.g.* Excursion 6.6A); careful mapping and granulometric analysis by Ablay *et al.* (1995) have shown that the ~2 ky eruption developed into a sub-plinian eruption with a column height of 15-20 km. The later red, less inflated pumice was considered by Ablay *et al.* (1995) to be the product of vulcanian blasts associated with late lava dome emplacement (unit III), and breadcrust bombs of similar material on the slopes of Montaña Blanca reinforce this interpretation. This story is taken up again in Excursion 8.2.

Around 10.0km the road passes through a shiny-black phonolitic obsidian flow field from Montaña Rajada, but it is not easy to pull off to examine it closely here. East of the road it banks up against Montaña Mostaza.

Stop 6.5 (11.3km): Montaña Mostaza breached scoria cone **

Shortly after km post 36 is a place where two cars can pull off on the right hand side, providing a view point to examine the **breached** basaltic scoria cone of Montaña Mostaza, one of the few basaltic strombolian centres within the caldera ring fracture. The lava flow responsible for the breach extends to the SE, but its proximal portion has been covered by a later trachyphonolite flow from Los Corrales on the NW side of the road. The distal apron of the flow can be seen on Excursion 6.6B.

Drive northeast and park at the Visitor Centre (14.5km).

Stop 6.6 (14.3 km): Walks from the Visitor Centre

Two alternative walks are possible from the Visitor Centre carpark. It is not feasible to combine both walks with the stops listed above during a single day.

Figure 29. Transition (in the foreground) from unwelded pumice fall - lower right - to rheomorphic welded fallout deposit above at La Fortaleza (Excursion 6.6A). Columnar-jointed cliffs of lava-like welded fallout facies are seen in the middle ground. The gentler slope below the cliffs consists of Lower Group lavas of the Tigaiga massif, exposed in the northern segment of the caldera wall.

Day 6. Las Cañadas caldera

Excursion 6.6A. La Fortaleza welded phonolitic pumice fallout and the northern caldera wall

The walk to La Fortaleza takes about 45-50 minutes each way. Start on the paved path to the left of the steps down to the Visitor Centre exhibition, signed to Rutas 1 and 6 (see official *Mappa del Parque Nacional del Teide*). The path leads up and down over flow-fronts and lobes of phonolite lavas, mainly from Montaña Blanca, liberally covered with Montaña Blanca grey-green pumice (~2 ka eruption) and coarser brown pumice (see Stop 6.4). Where the path divides, take the branch marked '1' which continues to the impressive columnar-jointed red wall of La Fortaleza (the '6' branch leads left to ascend Montaña Blanca). The path descends from a Montaña Blanca flow-front on to a pumice-covered alluvial plain. The peak on the right (El Cabezon) consists of pre-caldera Lower Group lavas (Martí *et al.* 1994) that belong to the Tigaiga massif, an isolated remnant of the Cañadas edifice that has withstood landsliding. The SW face of El Cabezon is a stretch of the northern sector of the caldera wall; the missing segment between El Cabezon and El Portillo has been removed by the Orotava valley landslide. The same lavas form the lower part of La Fortaleza to the left, but its upper cliff consists of intensely welded and columnar-jointed younger phonolitic fallout deposits of the Diego Hernandez Formation, similar to, but probably younger than, those capping other sectors of the caldera rim, *e.g.* at Guajara (Day 7).

Follow the cairns up to the col between the two hills (shrine, picnic tables). Turn left and follow the base of the cliffs westward to the first prominent rib from which the entire length of La Fortaleza face can be seen. The evidence for La Fortaleza being a welded fallout deposit rather than an ignimbrite can be seen at the base of this rib. Beside a felled tree-stump are recognizable pumice fall deposits which, though somewhat lithified, show negligible welding. These pass upward (Figure 29) into progressively more strongly welded rocks (showing **fiamme**) and then into swirly flow-banded rheomorphic and lava-like phonolites that form the jointed main portion of the cliff. It is this transition, from unwelded phonolitic pumice-fall deposits to lava-like rheomorphic deposits that led Martí *et al.* (1995) and Soriano *et al.* (2002 – see figs. 3D and 6) to interpret the massive welded phonolitic deposits of the caldera rim as proximal, late-plinian fountaining fallout deposits (*cf.* Figure 33) rather than welded ignimbrites from pyroclastic flows.

Does the existence here of proximal welded fallout deposits similar to those capping other sectors of the caldera rim suggest that the magma erupted from ring-fracture-controlled vents nearby? This is important evidence favouring caldera formation by vertical rather than lateral collapse.

The summit of La Fortaleza can easily be climbed from the shrine col, and offers excellent views round the missing sector of the caldera wall. Across the alluvial plain below, a late Montaña Blanca lava, reddish in colour, can be seen to have flowed over an earier grey one (probably from a vent on Montaña de los Corrales). A row of small vents running up the flanks of Teide – Las Lajas – has been the site for flank eruptions of Teide phonolitic lavas.

Excursion 6.6B. Montaña de las Arenas Negras and the Diego Hernandez Formation

This walk along the foot of the NE **topographic caldera wall** takes about 60 minutes each way. Walk south along the barred 'pista forestal', forking right where it starts to ascend to the caldera rim and passing a barrier restricting vehicle access.

As noted from stop 5.11 and shown in Figure 23, a cluster of **scoria cones** occurs in this corner of the caldera, including the aptly named Montaña de Arenas Negras (i.e. 'black sands'). Most – excluding Montaña de la Mostaza – are closely associated with the caldera wall, and may indicate where the caldera ring fracture intersected (or has since been exploited by) the late-Dorsal basaltic magma plumbing system, just as necks and plugs seen on Excursion 7.1 possibly mark where the **structural caldera margin** intersects the more evolved Cañadas or Teide-Pico Viejo magma chamber.

Continue along the track, flanking the basalt flow that has issued from the Montaña de la Mostaza cone. A prominent set of vertical dykes (Figure 30, left-hand side) marks the beginning of the remarkable Diego Hernandez sector of the caldera wall. Here the caldera wall intersects what is interpreted as an infilled radial palaeovalley on the upper flanks of the pre-caldera Cañadas volcano – at the point where it meets the Cordillera Dorsal – in which are preserved the closing stages of the Cañadas volcanic stratigraphy (Table 2): the Diego Hernandez Formation of Martí *et al.* (1994) emplaced between 540 and 170 ka. The succession is predominantly felsic, and is subdivided by means of intervening basaltic horizons (lavas or scoria beds).

Figure 30. Panoramic view of the magnificent Diego Hernandez sector of the Las Cañadas caldera wall (Excursion 6.6B)

Day 6. Las Cañadas caldera

The cliffs exhibit the gamut of pyroclastic types: cross-bedded surge deposits and unwelded ignimbrites precominate, but pumice fall and flow deposits are common, as well as scoriaceous and accretionary lapilli and sedimentary beds formed by fluvial reworking.

The cliffs exhibit a diversity of pyroclastic deposits, including dark Strombolian scoria beds, pale massive unwelded ignimbrites, (some with dark streaky pumices resembling those seen at stop 5.1), lithic-rich ignimbrites, darker compositionally stratified ignimbrites, pumice fall deposits, beds of accretionary lapilli, and sedimentary beds formed by fluvial reworking. From the track the sequence can be best appreciated by making a composite log from the track with the aid of binoculars. *N.B. The cliffs are a 'reserve area' and should not be climbed without prior permission from the Park office in La Orotava (see p.67).* The reader is referred to the many excellent pictures of the cliffs in Araña & Coello (1989; pp201-6).

Day 7. Guajara and the eastern sector of the caldera rim

Day 7. Guajara and a traverse round the eastern sector of the caldera rim

The complete high-level walk along the rim of the eastern caldera wall is a magnificent scenic experience, second only to the ascent of Teide itself, and offers insights into the origins of the massive ramparts of welded phonolitic tuffs that adorn the caldera rim. However it should be undertaken only by fit, experienced hill-walkers under favourable weather conditions. Allow at least 7 hours of daylight for the complete walk, plus an additional 90 minutes if you plan to climb Guajara (2715m, the highest point on the caldera rim) *en route*. Those undertaking the walk should equip themselves for a physically demanding walk through remote country: take ample reserves food, plenty of water, sun protection and appropriate clothing for the season, first-aid kit, bivouac bag and so on. This walk should never be attempted alone.

Figure 31. View from the summit of Guajara (Excursion 7.1) of Montaña Blanca and Montaña Rajada, with the late lava coulée of El Culaton nestling between them (Figure 28a) and the lava platform of El Tabonal Negro spreading in front of them. The eruptive fissure for the ~2ka BP sub-plinian eruption can be clearly seen on Montaña Blanca, with the brown coulée of clastogenic lava issuing from it (Stop 8.2f). Note that late black phonolitic lava flows from Teide postdate the reddish pumice fall blanket that marked the end of the ~2ka eruption.

Day 7. Guajara and the eastern sector of the caldera rim

Excursion 7.1: Traverse of the caldera rim *** ^^^

The excursion begins at the carpark at the end of the Piedra access road SE of the Parador; this is a turn on the right, 400m *before* the Roques de Garcia carpark turn, as one drives north on the TF-21. The full walk ends near El Portillo visitor centre, at the NE entrance to the caldera, and *arrangements need to be planned for transport back to the starting point*: the winter bus service ceases mid-afternoon; a 'there-and-back' walk as far as Montaña Pasajiron would provide a worthwhile and informative compromise, almost as strenuous but taking less time. Place names given below are from the 1:30,000 map of the Parque Nacional del Teide, obtainable from the information centre at the Parador, but this is not essential for the walk.

Set off along the dirt road from the gate, initially ascending onto the margins of the El Sanatorio caldera-floor phonolite lava dome, showing excellent a'a-like surface features. Piedras Amerillas, the first peak on the right, consists of thin, poorly sorted lithic-rich debris avalanche beds (mostly dipping into the caldera) similar to those of Roques de Garcia.

The track continues winding between the El Sanatorio lava dome to the left (Figure 23) and – judging from their irregular jointing – caldera-margin felsic necks and plugs cut by cone-sheets on the right; some may have served as conduits for the plinian eruptions whose products are seen in the Bandas del Sur. Pass a path turning off to the left, and descend on to an extensive plain floored by alluvium deposited from ephemeral lakes. The path up the caldera wall departs to the right at a 0.5m cairn. Zig-zag up the easily followed path, and, if intending to climb La Guajara, take a right branch up the upper wall, which allows inspection of pale pyroclastic deposits just below the top. These consist of unwelded and partially welded ignimbrites, the latter banking against darker pre-caldera lavas.

The approach to the summit of Guajara (2715m) leads across pumice fall beds, overlain by foliated welded rheomorphic pyroclastics of the Guajara Formation (Table 2) interpreted as products of fire fountaining (Martí *et al.* 1995). The summit platform however consists of welded rocks with smaller fiamme and a fine-grained matrix, ramping to the NE (dipping to SW) which Martí *et al.* (1995) interpret as a welded ignimbrite. Note the magnificent vews of Teide, Montaña Blanca (with the clastogenic lava flow cascading from the vent - *cf* Excursion 8.2), Montaña Rajada, El Tabonal Negro (Figures 28 and 31), Pico Viejo and the southern wall of the caldera (rear cover, lower picture). This is a good viewpoint to observe the complex age-relationships between successive generations of Montaña Blanca and Teide lavas.

On descending back to the col (Degollada de Guajara), note the vertically jointed strongly welded rampart (resting on white, bedded pumice fall beds) on the SW flank of Montaña de Pasajiron directly ahead. This relationship can be seen at various places along the caldera rim, as described in great detail by Soriano *et al.* (2002). Continue along the path that zig-zags up to the summit of Pasajiron, noting the changing views of Teide and Montaña Blanca (front cover), and of Gran Canaria to the southeast. From

Day 7. Guajara and the eastern sector of the caldera rim

Figure 32. Cliff of welded plinian fallout draping the caldera wall crest at Roque de la Grieta (Excursion 7.1). Note how the nearer unit thickens to the left (into the caldera).

the top, view the Roque de la Grieta ahead, showing an excellent section of clastogenic spatter accumulations draping over the caldera rim (Figure 32), thickening on the intra-caldera side. Careful logging at sites such as this has demonstrated that the welded rocks grade downward and laterally into well sorted pumice fall deposits (Soriano *et al.* 2002), indicating that the impressive ramparts of highly welded, often **rheomorphic** phonolite along this sector of the caldera rim are fall-out deposits from **fire-fountaining**, rather than welded ignimbrite (pyroclastic flow) deposits. These authors record a gradation from unwelded pumice fall, through moderately welded (*cf.* Figure 29) and strongly welded facies to a lava-like (rheomorphic) facies up to 15m thick in caldera-wall exposures, similar to the transition seen at La Fortaleza (Excursion 6.6A). The prevalence of welded fall deposits (a relatively rare occurrence among calc-alkaline pyroclastics) on the caldera rim and at Montaña Blanca (Figure 28, Stop 8.2a) is one of the most distinctive aspects of Tenerife volcanology. It reflects the abundance of relatively volatile-poor ('degassed') but alkali-rich[18] phonolite magma reaching the surface during the waning stages of plinian and sub-plinian eruptions from highly evolved alkaline magma cham-

---

[18] *See Fig. G1 in the Glossary.*

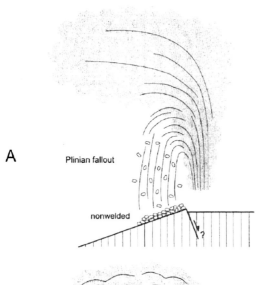

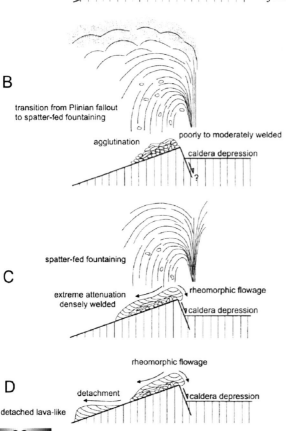

Figure 33. Evolution from plinian pumice fallout (unwelded pumice fall beds) to fountain-fed spatter and rheomorphic 'lava-like facies' during the waning stages of a plinian eruption, explaining the succession seen at La Fortaleza and on Montaña de Pasajiron. Reproduced from Soriano et al. (2002, fig. 8) with kind permission of the Geological Society of America.

bers (Figure 33). It is reasonable to suppose that the vents for such fountaining, like the volcanic necks noted earlier, lay close to the developing caldera margin.

The N and NE ramparts of Pasajiron are precipitous, and here the path deviates to the right (follow green paint spots and cairns) to descend safely to a clear wide track crossing a barranco on the eastern side. Alternatively, if time is limited, return directly to the car at this stage.

If continuing, the track provides a clear route until near to the end of the walk, and improves to a 4WD vehicle track further on. Note phonolitic spatter resting on unwelded pumice fall to the left of the track uphill from Montaña del Palo. More clearly defined pumice fall beds topped by welded spatter can be seen directly north of the same small peak (southern flank of Roque de la Grieta). Once past the major peaks, the track offers repeated panoramas across the caldera from different angles. The relatively flat terrain from here on is carpeted by three kinds of pyroclastic fall deposit:

3. fine basaltic scoria from one or more of the numerous cinder cones scattered over the south-western end of the Cordillera Dorsal, two of which – the Siete Fuentes (7 springs) and Fasnia cones seen from stop 5.10 – erupted in 1704-5 (Cabrera Lagunilla & Hernández-Pacheco, 1987);
2. coarser, less inflated reddish pumice;
1. grey-green, relatively fine pumice.

Figure. 34.   The Vilaflor 'ignimbrite': rheomorphic outflow facies of a late-plinian fallout spatter deposit seen from Stop 7.2.   Note the ramp structure dipping from right to left, picked out by afternoon sunshine.   Photo: D. Millward

Day 7. Guajara and the eastern sector of the caldera rim

Pumices types 1 and 2 resemble the Montaña Blanca stratigraphy seen at Stop 6.4, but mapping of that deposit by Ablay *et al.* (1995) showed it to be deposited mainly to the NE, not here to the east of Montaña Blanca. The source of the pumice fall blanket here is not clear.

After Roque Verde, one can see down to the Diego Hernandez cliff, in which a cross section of pyroclastic succession of the Diego Hernandez Formation (Martí *et al.* 1994) has been preserved in a palaeovalley (Figure 30). After this, the track winds among various scoria cones and their scoria blankets. After passing east of Montaña Colorada and over the Collada Degollada de Abreo, turn left across the alluvial plain of Llanos de Maja, turn right between the two Cerrillar cones (2343 and 2361m), then follow the path down to the road SW of the visitor centre.

Any daylight remaining on completion of this walk can be used for a brief inspection of a **rheomorphic** outflow analogue of the welded plinian fall phonolites seen on the caldera rim[19]. Drive back past the Roques to the junction of the TF-38 and TF-21 at Boca Tauce (*reset trip recorder here*). Turn left (TF-21 signed to Vilaflor). After 0.7km, pull off on a small lay-by on the left; look back down the road and see above it a magnificent section through unwelded ignimbrites and plinian fall deposits of the Ucanca Formation (Table 2), capped by cliffs of welded fallout facies similar to those of the Guajara Formation. Continue over the Los Roques de Ucanca pass (splendid views to La Gomera and El Hierro). Continue driving down toward Vilaflor until a left-hand bend where a wooden sign[20] beside a track on the right reads 'La Vica - sin salida' (= no exit). Park here.

Stop 7.2 (8.8 km fom Boca Tauce): *Vilaflor rheomorphic 'ignimbrite'*

On the inside of the bend (*pay attention to fast traffic*) are relatively fresh exposures of what has been described as the 'Vilaflor Ignimbrite' (Araña & Coello, 1989). The term 'ignimbrite', implying a pyroclastic *flow* deposit, is understandable given the appearance of wispy fiamme in this intensely welded and crudely jointed rock. However, in the light of the welded proximal fallout deposits seen on the caldera rim (at Guajara and at La Fortaleza, Excursion 6.6A), it is now accepted that this 30-40m thick body is also a product of late-plinian fire fountaining (Figure 30). It resembles the clastogenic 'lava-like facies' of Soriano *et al.* (2002), and looking at its outcrop on the opposite side of the next barranco downhill one can see through the trees a curviplanar foliation or **ramp structure** dipping into the hill (Fig. 34) similar to the ramping of a viscous lava flow front (*cf.* stop 6.3). This evidence of flowage, supported by smaller-scale folding of foliation, justifies the adjective **rheomorphic**.

---

[19] *However these exposures are better seen in morning light so could with advantage be visited on returning to the caldera the following day.*
[20] *Legible only to traffic heading toward Vilaflor.*

Day 7. Guajara and the eastern sector of the caldera

It is worthwhile to walk 50-100m down the La Vica track to a viewpoint beside a building. There are magnificent views from here over the southern flanks of the island towards the Roque del Conde massif. One can pick out the alignment of flank-eruption basaltic scoria cones (*cf.* Martí *et al.* 1995 fig. 16).

Day 8. Teide, Montaña Blanca/Pico Viejo, and the historic eruptions of 1798 (Narices del Teide) and 1909 (Chinyero)

The ascent of Teide makes a fitting climax to the trip, but as it depends on good weather, particularly in the winter months, it may be advisable not to leave it to the last day of the tour. *Note also that access to the actual summit (Piton del Teide) is allowed only with a permit ('permiso') for each individual in the party, obtained in advance. Pico del Teide permits may be applied for online at http://bit.ly/2EVetKW.* You will be asked to nominate two consecutive dates (to allow for adverse weather) for your visit, and the time of day slot. The permit is *always* inspected by a Park ranger at the start of the summit path. This conspicuously bureaucratic step is evidently intended – with some justification – to restrict the total number visiting the summit. On winter days when the cable car is not working due to icing or wind, those who walk up (via the Montaña Blanca track) gain unhindered access to the summit.

If two or more cars are available, park one at the foot of the Montaña Blanca track (6.2 km from Roques de Garcia, between Stops 6.3 and 6.4). The remainder should park at the Teleférico. *Do not leave valuables in cars.*

Stop 8.1: *Teide peak (3718m)*

Though Teide can be climbed by foot starting at the Montaña Blanca carpark (4+ hours to summit: walkers must make allowance for the altitude), the least time-consuming approach is to take the Teleférico up (10 minutes + 20 minutes climb from the terminus to the summit) and then walk down (3 hours via Mta Blanca for the reasonably fit). The Teleférico costs ₠ 10 (one way) or ₠ 20 (return, 2003 prices). The Teleférico begins operating at 09.00 (arrive early to avoid long queues once coaches arrive) but it does not operate if the wind at the summit exceeds 45 km h^{-1} or if icing is a problem. Anyone ascending in winter should be equipped for bitterly cold wind; in some winters the snow cover is also extensive, and prior advice should be sought at the teleférico station (Tel 922 69 40 38) or the Visitor Centre (Figures 23 & 28).

The ascent offers magnificent views of the Cañadas caldera floor and most of the length of the wall. Note also the SE-trending eruptive fissure on Montaña Blanca (MB) that fed the ~2ka eruption, from which coulées of **clastogenic** have flowed down the southern flanks. From the last pylon to the upper station, the teleférico crosses a relatively flat area (see Figure 25) marking the location of two earlier summit

---

[21] *Those intending to walk down via Montaña Blanca or Pico Viejo may wish also to seek permission to visit the MB eruptive fissure (Excursion 8.2) or the Pico Viejo caldera floor (Excursion 8.3).*

Figure 35. View from the Teide cable-car towards the NE showing the Oratava valley wreathed in cloud. On the right is the Cordillera Dorsal with the Old Basalt 'Series'' hills of Anaga in the far distance.

craters. The first crater was about 1km in diameter, the second was formed by the destruction of a second cone that formed within it, and the current cone, El Pitón, has been constructed on lavas infilling these earlier craters.

From the cable car station, the panorama of the caldera to the south and east is superb, and one also gains a view of the 1704/5 cones of Volcán Fasnia and other fissure-fed cones that are not visible from the foot of the wall. Cloud permitting, the large island of Gran Canaria is usually visible: it is difficult to believe it is 90km away.

For visitors intending to descend by cable car, the following easy walks are available from the upper cable car station. Routes for those wishing to walk down are described under excursions 8.2 and 8.3 below.

A. *Track to the mirador overlooking Pico Viejo* (45 minutes return). Walk underneath the cable car cables and follow the marked, roughly paved path (Sendero de Pico Viejo, no 12) past a volcanic-gas monitoring station. The mirador offers glorious views (similar to the back cover, top picture) of Pico Viejo to the west with La Gomera and El Hierro beyond, and (to NW) to the Teno massif with La Palma beyond. Note the pumice deposit from the ~2ka PV eruption covering the shoulder leading to Pico Viejo. Several Recent scoria cones can be seen on the slopes between Pico Viejo and Teno, including La Chinyero, the source of the 1909 basalt flow, the most recent eruption on Tenerife. This NW zone of post-caldera basaltic activity has been referred to as the Santiago Rift (Ablay & Kearey, 2000) but there is negligible structural evidence for extension here.

B. *Track to the summit of Piton del Teide*[22]. The ascent takes 20-30 minutes up for the reasonably fit and 15 minutes down. Follow the path round the front of the service building (toilets) and walk a few more metres to where the path divides, the left turn leading to the summit (path numbered 10); visitors without permits for the summit will be turned back by park wardens at this point. The track mostly follows the main channel of a glassy phonolite lava, partially emptied leaving behind upstanding levées - note the smooth internal surface. As the summit is approached, rock surfaces take on a 'salty' look, and red clays indicate the increasing intensity of hydrothermal alteration. Note the fumaroles in and around the summit crater, depositing yellow sulphur and white alunite $[KAl_3(SO_4)_2(OH)_6]$. The views from the summit are incomparable (upper photo, back cover). Features noted under walks A and C may also be noted from the summit.

C. *Track to the mirador overlooking the north coast* (20-25 minutes return). Start out as under route B, but turn right through a narrow gap in the levée of a late Teide phonolite flow at the point where the summit path turns left (take the path numbered 11). Note the feeble fumarole steaming on the right near to the Montaña Blanca turn. The mirador view to the northeast shows the Cordillera Dorsal and the ranges of the Anaga massif beyond. To the north is the prominent columnar-jointed red phonolite rampart of La Fortaleza (Excursion 6.6A), a remnant of the northern sector of the caldera wall, with the landslip-carved valley of La Orotava beyond (Figure 35), and the Anaga massif in the far distance. To the northwest is a broad valley in which the town of Icod is situated; the town lies barely 0.5km west of the major Recent phonolitic lava coulées of Roques Blancos (Araña & Coello, 1989, pp. 227-233), which erupted high on the northwest slopes of Pico Viejo (Figure 23) and flowed into the sea; the levées can be picked out from the summit of Teide. The island of La Palma is often visible to the west-northwest beyond the dramatic ridges and ravines of the Teno massif.

The following paragraph is not part of walk C. A feast of volcanology awaits those who choose to walk down to the road, whichever route they take. Both routes involve tracks over very rugged terrain (especially Excursion 8.3 – see the caution at the start of that paragraph) and long walks back to vehicles left at the lower cable car

---

[22] *Access to the actual summit of Pico del Teide (as opposed to the cable car station) requires a 'permiso' – see details given at start of Day 8.*

Figure 36. View from the upper part of the track down from the summit cable-car station to Montaña Blanca (Excursion 8.2). Beyond the pumice-covered summit of Montaña Blanca (bottom right) can be seen the late lava coulée (unit III in Figure 28b) of El Culaton, the summit lava coulées of Montaña Rajada and its dark obsidian lava flows beyond, various caldera-floor domes and flows, the Diego Hernandez and Angastura sectors of the caldera wall, and the AD 1705 cones of Volcán de Fasnia and Siete Fuentes on the caldera rim.

station; do not attempt these routes if you are not a properly equipped, experienced mountain walker; give yourself plenty of daylight time.

Excursion 8.2: Montaña Blanca (MB)

This walk via MB (Sendero no 7) takes 2-4 hours to reach the road, depending on detours made *en route* (Figure 28). The path leads from a point 100m short of the north coast mirador above (route C), and down the axis of a phonolite obsidian flow erupted from the Piton del Teide (according to Carracedo & Day, 2003, the correlation with a historic eruption seen in 1492 has now been discredited). A magnificent panorama unfolds (Figure 36): phonolite lava coulées on the top and flanks of Montaña Rajada (MR) lightly coated with pumice, a later flow not covered by pumice that has issued from the col between MR and MB (El Culaton, Figures 28a and Fig. 31), the caldera wall, the Cordillera Dorsal capped by Recent and historic scoria cones and Gran Canaria beyond.

Day 8. Teide, Montaña Blanca/Pico Viejo

Figure 37. Welded fallout spatter from the Montaña Blanca ~2ka eruption, beside the path down from Teide (Stop 8.2a).

Below the Refuge, the path passes on to scree-slopes of brownish ~2ka pumice that predate the Teide obsidian flows on either side but which were laid down on an older flow beneath. Approaching the Montaña Blanca plateau (Stop 8.2a in Figure 28a, 50m above the vehicle track), note that pumice (brownish here) locally shows signs of welding (Figure 37). Welding becomes intense with **rheomorphic** flow-folds at 8.2b, beside the track leading to the summit of MB. Ablay *et al.* (1995) attribute these welded deposits to late fire-fountain spatter from the Montaña Blanca fissure which, judging from the example at location 8.2a, probably extended some distance up the slopes of Teide before being covered by post-2ka Teide lava. Note that the pumice and agglutinate are virtually aphyric, easily distinguished from the strongly feldspar-phyric Teide lavas.

At the foot of the steep descent, note the rounded blocks of obsidian ('Huevos del Teide' = Teide's eggs) that have rolled down from the front of the recent obsidian flow. Here one turns right to ascend the rounded dome of Montaña Blanca – an excellent viewpoint to review the stratigraphy of the MB centre (8.2c in Figure 28a). Look back from the track to see the black Piton del Teide flow off to the north confined between clear levées. The rounded slopes of Montaña Blanca are mantled by a thin deposit of brownish MB pumice belonging unit III in Figure 28b, resting on proximal green pumice from the main MB eruption (unit IIA).

Day 8. Teide, Montaña Blanca/Pico Viejo

Ablay *et al.* (1995) described the ~2ka eruption in some detail. Eruption occurred from vents on both MB and Pico Viejo (PV) and a similar succession is seen around both vents. When the eruption began, the lava-dome edifice of MB had already been constructed, and subsidence of the PV caldera had already taken place. From the distribution and characteristics of the MB Pumice, Ablay *et al.* (1995) concluded that the MB eruption was sub-plinian with an eruption column height of around 15-20 km and a mass eruption rate of 10^7 kg s^{-1}. Discharged from vents along the MB fissure (as seen from the cable car), this produced the extensive carpet of green pumice noted at Stop 6.4 and at La Fortaleza on Excursion 6.6A. The eruption is believed to have lasted 7-11 hours (similar to Mt St Helens in May 1980) and the elongation of the pumice blanket to the NE suggests a wind from the SW of about 10 m s^{-1}. Toward the end of the eruption the explosivity declined and the style of eruption developed into entense fire-fountaining. The lower eruption column at this stage allowed proximal pumice to reach the ground at a higher temperature that during the sub-plinian phase (Figure 33) as recorded in the densely welded proximal facies seen around the summit of MB and lining the fissure (unit IIB in Fig.28b).

Those with permission to visit the ~2ka fissure (Stop 8.6f – see footnote 21) should follow an indistinct path leading to the south a few tens of metres along the MB summit track. This leads gently down southwards, close to the edge of a feldspar-phyric Teide obsidian flow that has been deflected southwards by the mass of MB. After about 200m the fissure will be seen on the left, trending SE (8.2d). Walk past two small lava domes of vitric phonolite (8.2e. belonging to unit III in Figure 28b) with concentric and radial fractures; note the association of red poorly inflated pumice. Continue along the fissure noting accumulations of poorly compacted phonolite spatter. to the top of the lava coulée (8.2f – also clearly seen in the front cover picture). There is a transition down slope from welded spatter to a clastogenic obsidian lava flow exceeding one metre in thickness in places, which has evidently flowed or slid over the underlying pumice lapilli (*cf.* Figure 33) covering the slope below.

To descend to the main road, return to the MB summit track, turn left and follow its many bends to the TF-21 (use of short-cuts is forbidden). Ten minutes or so before reaching the road, where the path has been cut into the hillside, note a bed of banded lava-like phonolitic spatter. A glance at the map (Figure 28a) shows this spot to be on the extension of the Montaña Blanca fissure (since covered by the late El Culaton coulée).

Excursion 8.3: Pico Viejo *** ^^^

This descent route is for the fit and agile only. Allow 6-7 hours of daylight for the descent to the road. Arrangements need to be made beforehand to be picked up at the Boca Tauce intersection between the TF-21 and the TF-38 where the descent route ends (Figure 23).

Figure 38 (above and above right - note overlap of two pictures). Panoramic view into the caldera of Pico Viejo seen from the ESE (Excursion 8.3). In shade, behind the figure on the left, is the southern caldera wall exposing massive **phonotephrite** *lava flows (see Figure 39). The 1798 explosion pit, whose ejecta cover most of the brown and grey portions of the caldera floor, can be seen mid-left in front of the lowest section of the caldera wall. The pinkish area on the right is floored by clastogenic Pico Viejo phonolite lava from the ~2ka eruption that has flowed down from the caldera rim, sparsely covered by late pumice fall from the same eruption. Towards the far wall are remnants of an earlier basanitic scoria cone, and pre-caldera basanite lavas can be seen on the right, cut by a mafic dyke. A map of the caldera can be found in Martí et al. (1995, figure 4).*

From the mirador overlooking Pico Viejo, take an initially indistinct path that leads from the parapet on the left side of the display board. The path leads down the left-hand side of a lava levée, sometimes visible as a gravelly path but often relying on frequent cairns to show the route across the desolate blocky flow terrain, covered by greenish Pico Viejo pumice lapilli, lightly covered with abundant larger brown pumice clasts as described for the MB centre (Stop 6.4). A clear path leads across the pumice field toward the left-hand (SE) rim of Pico Viejo. Note beyond a shoulder on the right a late post-pumice phonolite lava dome. Continue gently down to the left of the saddle, crossing an eruptive fissure that has produced accumulations of spatter and flow-banded clastogenic lava very similar to those of Montaña Blanca (path not very clear here). A clear trail leads on up to the eastern shoulder of Pico Viejo, from where a short diversion leads to the

caldera rim (Figure 38)[23].

The Pico Viejo caldera is a vertical collapse feature that exposes in its walls outward-dipping basanite and phonotephrite lavas of the Pico Viejo cone. The caldera is floored by sub-horizontal tephriphonolite lavas, and a remnant of this old caldera fill succession that has resisted subsidence also forms a facing along the southern wall (in shade in Figure 38). The floor is covered by (a) basaltic scoria from an intra-caldera cone, (b) a lobe of clastogenic phonolite lava from the ~2ka eruption that has flowed down from the eastern caldera rim, (c) pumice deposits from the same eruption, and (d) grey heterolithic ejecta from the 1798 explosion pit that occupies the western corner.

The relationships and differences betwen Teide and Pico Viejo eruptive styles and products can be discussed here (note the several black vitric phonolite flows that can be seen cascading down from Teide across the carpet of about 2ka BP pumice). One can also ponder the magma plumbing system that fed similar eruptive cycles and products approximately 2000 years ago from vents *on either side of Teide (i.e.* Pico Viejo and Montaña Blanca) without apparently erupting from Teide itself.

There is no easy way down to the road. The route shown on the official *Mappa del*

---

[23] *The floor of the Pico Viejo caldera is a reserve area, and permission is required from the Parque office in La Orotava (see p.67) before climbing down to it (accessed from the eastern side).*

Day 8. Teide, Montaña Blanca/Pico Viejo

Parque Nacional del Teide descends westward above the Narices del Teide (a basaltic centre that erupted in 1798) to join the TF38 near to the Narices mirador. However it may be easier to descend east of the Narices to the black scoria field on its SE side, from where a zig-zag path descends across scoria to a vehicle track that provides endlessly meandering but easy access to the Boca Tauce road junction. See Update 7.

The remaining stops, for those who have time, lie along the TF-38 road from Boca Tauce to Chio. They can be visited as conveniently on another day, so distances are given here both from Boca Tauce (TF-38 / TF-21 junction) and from the Chio intersection (TF-38 / TF-82 junction).

Stop 8.4 (3.1km from Boca Tauce; 25.1km from TF-82): *1798* Chahorra eruption *

Immediately after the Vilaflor junction, the TF-38 Chio road passes for a distance of 2.5km over this historic a'a basanite flow from Chahorra *(= Narices del Teide)* and crosses another narrower tongue 1.5km later, shortly after the Narices mirador (3.1km from Boca Tauce) which gives an excellent view of the Narices with an explanatory display). Locally some restricted lava channels contain a small amount of pahoehoe lava.

Stop 8.5 (14.6 km from Boca Tauce; 13.6km from TF-82): Chinyero 1909 eruption ** ^

The 80m-high Chinyero cone, from which lava now covering 2.2km^2 was erupted in 1909, is accessible (signed) from the TF-38 Chio road close to the most northerly of the main bends. This is a typical strombolian cone of **basanite** composition; the thickness of deposit in the cone can be estimated. Note that a covering of black scoria extends beyond the cone, rapidly decreasing in thickness and clast size with distance from the vent.

Stop 8.6 (18.2 km from Boca Tauce; 10.3 km from TF-82): Drained lava tube **

Opposite a track on the right signed Posta Cueva de los Pajaros is the largest of several examples of drained lava tubes seen along the lower parts of this road (Figure 24). This has a skylight on its northern side; sections of the roof look very insecure and should be assessed before entering.

Other places worth visiting

Anyone driving eastward along the north coast from Icod to Puerto de la Cruz might wish to visit the following two localities (Stops 9.1 and 9.2). Excursion 9.3 provides an easy but scenic high-level walk of volcanological interest.

Stop 9.1 Debris avalanche deposit **

Carracedo and Day (2002) describe a locality in the north of the island along the TF-42 where a debris avalanche deposit similar to those flooring the Orotava and Güimar valleys can be seen at a road-side exposure. 5km E of the turn to San Juan de la Rambla and 3km E of the Barranco de Ruiz, there is a roadcut in thick debris avalanche deposit, just before the left turn to Playa de Socorro. (Caution: busy road - pay attention to traffic.)The exposure shows 'sheared blocks of lava and pumiceous phonolite breccia, up to 10m across, in a massive, relatively coarse-grained matrix' typical of distal debris avalanche deposits. Comparison may be made with the avalanche deposit constituting the Roques de Garcia (Stop 6.1).

Stop 9.2 Montaña de la Horca 1430AD basanite volcano *

The TF-5 motorway passes (travelling eastward) through a cone of the 1430 AD eruption, Montaña de los Frailes, 2km after emerging from the road-tunnel beneath Los Realejos (km post 42), immediately before the exit for San Jeronimo, but one cannot stop to examine it. Instead, leave at this exit and head north. Turn right at the T-junction (TF-320) and continue eastward. After just over 1km turn left toward Puerto de la Cruz (TF-312). Turn right immediately for the mirador on Montaña de la Horca, a second cone of the same eruption.

Excursion 9.3 Sombrero de Chasna walk (near Vilaflor) *** ^^

A short but very scenic walk, especially attractive with orographic stratus cloud below. 9.5km up the TF-21 from the café/petrol station junction S of Vilaflor, park beside ruined cabins with painted white arrows on them beside the main road. Follow trail arrows marked 'TS10', initially southwards, on the east side of road. Where the paths divide 10 minutes after starting, follow white dots (not arrows) up on to a relatively open plateau. Follow the well marked trail (white spots and cairns) across one water course then climb the next to the east, all the way up to the caldera rim (wonderful view of Teide and Pico Viejo) directly beneath the impressive red jointed cliffs of El Sombrero de Chasna, which glow brilliant red in early evening sunshine. Examine the cliffs for evidence of a transition from unwelded pumice fall to rheomorphic fall-out spatter deposit as seen on Excursion 6.6A and 7.1. The return walk takes 1.5-2.0 hours.

ACKNOWLEDGEMENTS

We wish to thank Mike Branney for discussions on the Arico ignimbrite, for carefully reviewing parts of the manuscript and for advice on pyroclastic processes generally, and the late Laurie Doyle for comments on an early draft of this edition. We warmly acknowledge the many insights and contributions of our first-edition co-authors – Dave Millward, Giz Marriner, Mike Norry, Andy Saunders and Joán Martí – that have found their way into the new edition, and we thank the other colleagues who have accompanied us on subsequent trips and shared their ideas, particularly Joel Baker, Mary Gee and Tony Watts.

We are grateful to Elsevier Science Publishers BV for permission to reproduce Figure 2 and Figure 4 from the papers cited in the captions, and to the Geological Society of America for permission to reproduce Figure 33.

The printing costs for the guide were generously defrayed by a grant from the Curry Fund of the Geologists' Association.

FURTHER READING

ABLAY, G.J., AND KEAREY, P., 2000. Gravity constraints on the structure and volcanic evolution of Tenerife,Canary Islands. *J. geophys. Res.* **105** (B3), 5783-5796.

ABLAY, G.J., ERNST, G.G.J., MARTÍ, J., AND SPARKS, R.S.J., (1995). The 2020y BP subplinian eruption of Montaña Blanca, Tenerife. *Bulletin of Volcanology* **57**, 337-355.

ABLAY, G.J., CARROLL, M.R., PALMER, M.R., MARTÍ, J., AND SPARKS, R S J., 1998. Basanite-phonolite lineages of the Teide-Pico Viejo volcanic complex, Tenerife, Canary Islands. *J. Petrol.*, 905-36.

ALONSO, J.J., ARAÑA, V., AND MARTÍ, J. 1988. La ignimbrita de Arico (Tenerife). Mecanismo de emisión y de emplazamiento. *Revista de la Sociedad Geológica de España* **1**, 15-24. [MA 91M/0985]

ANCOCHEA, E., FÚSTER, J.M.,., IBARROLA, E., CENDRERO, A., COELLO, J., HERNÁN, F., CANTAGREL, J.M., AND JAMOND, C.,1990. Volcanic evolution of the island of Tenerife in the light of new K-Ar data. *J. Volcanol. geotherm. Res.* **44**, 231-249.

ANCOCHEA, E., CANTAGREL, J.M., FÚSTER, J.M., HUERTAS, M.J., AND ARNAUD, N.O., 1998. Vertical and lateral collapse on Tenerife (Canary Islands) and other volcanic ocean islands: comment. *Geology*, **24**, 861-2.

ANCOCHEA, E., HUERTAS, M.J., CANTAGREL, J.M., COELLO, J., FÚSTER, J.M., ARNAUD, N., AND IBARROLA, F., 1999. Evolution of the Cañadas edifice and its implications for the origin of the Cañadas caldera (Tenerife, Canary Islands). *J. Volcanol. geotherm. Res.* **88**, 177-99.

ANGUITA, F., AND HERNÁN, F.,1975. A propagating fracture model versus hotspot origin for the Canary Islands. *Earth Planet. Sci Letters* **27**, 11-19.

ARAÑA, V., AND COELLO, J. (editors) 1989. *Los volcanes y la caldera del Parque Nacional del Teide, Tenerife.* ICONA, Serie Técnica, Madrid. (Available on Inter-Library Loan.)

BOOTH, B., 1973. The Granadilla pumice deposit of southern Tenerife, Canary Islands. *Proc. Geol. Assoc.* **84**, 353-70.

BRANNEY, M.J., AND KOKELAAR, P., 1992. A reappraisal of ignimbrite emplacement: progressive aggradation and changes from particulate to non-particulate flow during emplacement of high-grade ignimbrite. *Bulletin of Volcanology.* **54**, 504-20.

BRANNEY, M.J., AND KOKELAAR, P., 2003. Pyroclastic density currents and the sedimentation of ignimbrites. *Geol. Soc. London Memoir* **27**, 130pp

BROWN, R.J., BARRY, T.L., BRANNEY, M.J., PRINGLE, M.S., AND BRYAN, S.E., 2003. The Quaternary pyroclastic succession of southeast Tenerife, Canary Islands: explosive eruptions, related caldera subsidence and sector collapse. *Geol Mag.* **140**, 265-88.

BRYAN, S., MARTÍ, J., AND CAS, R.A.F. 1998. Stratigraphy of the Bandas del Sur

Further reading

Formation: an extracaldera record of Quaternary phonolitic explosive eruptions from the Las Cañadas edifice, Tenerife (Canary Islands). *Geol. Mag.* **135**, 605-636.

BRYAN, S., CAS, R.A.F. AND MARTÍ, J., 2000. The 0.57 Ma plinian eruption of the Granadilla Member, Tenerife (Canary Islands): an example of complexity in eruption dynamics and evolution. *J. Volcanol. geotherm. Res.* **103**, 209-38.

BRYAN, S., MARTÍ, J., AND LEOSSON, M. 2002. Petrology and geochemistry of the Bandas del Sur Formation, Las Cañadas edifice, Tenerife (Canary Islands). *J. Petrol.* **43**, 1815-56.

CABRERA LAGUNILLA, M.P., AND HERNÁNDEZ-PACHECO, A. 1987. Las erupciones históricas de Tenerife (Canarias) en sus aspectos vulcanológico, petrológico y geoquiímico. *Revista de Materiales y Procesos Geológicos* **5**, 143-182. [MA 88M/6236]

CANTAGREL, J.M., ARNAUD, N.O., ACOCHEA, E., FÚSTER, J.M., AND HUERTAS, M.J., 1999. Repeated debris avalanches on Tenerife and genesis of the Las Cañadas caldera wall (Canary Islands). *Geology.* **27**, 739-42.

CARRACEDO, J-C., 1994. The Canary Islands: an example of structural control on the growth of large ocean-island volcanoes. *J. Volcanol. Geotherm. Res.* **60**, 225-41

CARRACEDO, J-C., AND DAY, S., 2002 *Classic Geology in Europe 4: Canary Islands.* Terra Press.

CARRACEDO, J-C., DAY, S., GUILLOU, H., RODRÍGUEZ BADIOLA, E., CANAS, J.A., AND PÉREZ TORRADO, F.J., 1998. Hotspot vlcanism close to a passive continental margin: the Canary Islands. *Geol. Mag.* **135**, 591-604.

CAS, R.A.F., AND WRIGHT, J.V., 1987. *Volcanic successions - ancient and modern.* London: Allen and Unwin.

FISHER, R.V., AND SCHMINCKE, H.-U., 1984. *Pyroclastic Rocks.* Berlin: Springer-Verlag.

FISHER, R.V., HEIKEN, G., AND HULEN, J.B. *et al.*, 1997. *Volcanoes - crucibles of change.* Princeton University Press.

FRANCIS, P., 1993. *Volcanoes - a planetary perspective.* Oxford.

FÚSTER, J.M., ARAÑA, V., BRANDLE, J., NAVARRO, J., ALONSO, U., AND APARICIO, A. 1968. *Geología y volcanología de las Islas Canarias: Tenerife.* Madrid: Instituto "Lucas Mallada" (Consejo Superior de Investigaciones Cientificas) 218 pp. Publication includes a full English translation.

GILL, , R., THIRLWALL, M., MARRINER, G., MILLWARD, D., NORRY, M., SAUNDERS, A., AND MARTÍ, J., 1994. *Tenerife, Canary Islands.* Geologists' Association Guide No. 49.

HAWKESWORTH, C.J., BLAKE, S., EVANS, P., HUGHES, R., MACDONALD, R., THOMAS, L.E., AND TURNER, S.P., 2000. Time scales of crystal fractionation in magma chambers - integrating physical, isotopic, and geochemical perspectives. *J. Petrol.* **41**, 991-1006.

Further reading

HOERNLE, K., AND SCHMICKE, H.-U., 1993. The role of partial melting in the 15-Ma geochemical evolution of Gran Canaria: a blob model for the Canary hotspot. *J. Petrol.* **34**, 599-626.

HUERTAS, M.J., ARNAUD, N.O., ANCOCHEA, E., CANTAGREL, J.M., AND FOSTER, J.M., 2002. $^{40}Ar/^{39}Ar$ stratigraphy of pyroclastic units from the Cañadas volcanic edifice (Tenerife, Canary Islands) and their bearing on the structural evolution. *J. Volcanol. Geotherm Res.* **115**, 351-365.

HÜRLIMANN, M., LEDESMA, A., AND MARTÍ, J., 1999. Conditions favouring catastrophic landslides on Tenerife (Canary Islands). *Terra Nova* **11**, 106-11.

KEATING, B.H., AND McGUIRE, W.J., 2000. Island edifice failures and associated tsunami hazards *Pure and Applied Geophysics* **157**, 899-955.

KRASTEL, S., SCHMINCKE, H.-U., JACOBS, C.L., RIHM, R., LE BAS, T.P., ALIBÉS, B., 2001. Submarine landslides around the Canary Islands. *J. geophys. Res.* **106**, 3977-97.

LE MAITRE, R.W., (editor) 2002. *Igneous rocks – a classification and glossary of terms.* 2nd edition. Cambridge University Press.

MARTÍ, J., MITJAVILA, J., AND ARAÑA, V., 1994. Stratigraphy, structure and geochronology of the Las Cañadas caldera (Tenerife, Canary Islands). *Geol. Mag.* **131**, 715-727.

MARTÍ, J., MITJAVILA, J., (EDITORS) 1995. *A field guide to the Central Volcanic Complex of Tenerife (Canary Islands).* Servicio de Publicaciones, Cabildo Insular de Lanzarote (Island Council of Lazarote). ISBN 84-87021-27-1.

MARTÍ, J., ABLAY, J., BRYAN, S., AND MITJAVILA, J. (1995). A field trip to the central volcanic complex of Tenerife: description of stops. In: Martí and Mitjavila (1995), 93-156.

MARTÍ, J., HURLIMANN, M., ABLAY, G.J., AND GUDMUNDSSON, A., 1997. Vertical and lateral collapses on Tenerife (Canary Islands) and other volcanic ocean islands. *Geology* **25**, 879-82.

MARTÍ, J., AND GUDMUNDSSON, A., 2000. The Las Cañadas caldera (Tenerife, Canary Islands): example of an overlapping collapse caldera generated by magma-chamber migration. *J. Volcanol. Geothermal Res.* **103**, 161-73.

MASSON, D., WATTS, A.B., GEE, M.J.R., URGELES, R., MITCHELL, N.C., LE BAS, T.P., CANALS, M. 2002. Slope failures on the flanks of the western Canary Islands. *Earth-Science Reviews.* **57**, 1-35.

NEUMANN, E.-R., WULFF-PEDERSEN, E., SIMONSEN, S.L., PEARSON, N.J., MARTÍ, J., AND MITJAVILA, J., 1999. Evidence for fractional crystallization of periodically refilled magma chambers in Tenerife, Canary Islands. *J Petrol.* **40**, 1089-1123.

RIDLEY, W.I., 1972. The field relations of the Las Cañadas volcanoes, Tenerife, Canary Islands. *Bull. Volc.* **35**318-34.

RIHN, R., JACOBS, C.L., KRASTEL, S., SCHMINCKE, H.-U. AND ALIBES, B., 1998. Las Hijas seamounts – the next Canary Island? *Terra Nova* **10**, 121-5.

ROTHERY, D.A. 2001. *Teach Yourself Volcanoes.* Hodder and Stoughton.

Further reading

SCHMINCKE, H.-U. 1987. *Geological field guide of Gran Canaria*. Pluto Press.

SORIANO, C., ZAFRILLA, S., MARTI, J., BRYAN, S., CAS, R. AND ABLAY, G. (2002). Welding and rheomorphism of phonolitic fallout deposits from the Las Cañadas caldera, Tenerife, Canary Islands. *Geological Society of America Bulletin* **114** 883-895.

SPARKS, R.S.J., SELF, S., AND WALKER, G.P.L., 1973. Products of ignimbrite eruptions. *Geology* **1,** 115-18.

TEIDE GROUP. 1987. Morphometric interpretation of the northwest and southeast slopes of Tenerife, Canary Islands. *J. geophys. Res.* **102**, 20325-42.

THIRLWALL, M.F., SINGER, B.S., AND MARRINER, G.F., 2000. ^{39}Ar-^{40}Ar ages and geochemistry of the basaltic shield stage of Tenerife, Canary Islands, Spain. *J. Volc. geotherm. Res.* **103**, 247-297.

THORPE, R., AND BROWN, G.C. 1991. *The field description of igneous rocks*. J. Wiley.

WATTS, A.B., AND MASSON, D.G., 1995. A giant landslide on the north flank of Tenerife, Canary Islands. *J. geophys. Res.* **100**, 24,487-98.

Appendix: Glossary of volcanological terms

a'a (pron. 'ah-ah') Hawaiian word for the form of basalt lava flow that has a vesicular, clinkery, rubbly upper surface.

accretionary lapilli pea-sized spheroidal concretions in a pyroclastic fall, flow or surge deposit that are formed by accretion of moist volcanic ash from an eruption column, due either to atmospheric moisture during an eruption or to phreatic or phreatomagmatic explosion.

ankaramite a type of basalt (usually alkali basalt) notably rich in clinopyroxene and olivine phenocrysts.

argon-argon dating 40Ar-39Ar dating is a variant of potassium-argon dating which, by releasing Ar and measuring its isotope ratio in a series of increments rather than in one step, allows systematic errors (to which conventional K-Ar dating is prone) to be detected and largely eliminated. The name derives from the other significant advance offerd by this method: K in the sample is converted into Ar by neutron bombardment in a nuclear reactor, allowing the daughter:parent ratio to be measured in a mass spectrometer as the isotope ratio 40Ar/39Ar.

ash fine-grained pyroclastic particles, smaller than 2mm.

ballistic pyroclastic bomb or block emplaced as a projectile, with a trajectory determined by its direction and momentum on exiting the vent.

basanite fine-grained basic or ultrabasic rock more alkaline than alkali basalt (see Fig. 39).

base surge a cool, moist pyroclastic surge associated with phreatic or phreatomagmatic explosions. Base surge deposits seen in cross-section (*e.g.* in a tuff-ring) are often characterized by antidune cross-bedding, reflecting the high energy of the current.

benmoreite a fine-grained intermediate volcanic rock of the alkali basalt-trachyte series (see Fig. 39 below); more evolved than mugearite, less evolved than trachyte.

block-and-ash flow deposit type of pyroclastic flow deposit that consists of a mixture of lithic blocks (sometimes quite large) and fine ash. A block-and-ash flow results from the collapse of a felsic lava dome, either under its own weight or as a result of overpressure of confined gases.

breached describing a scoria cone one side of which has failed. Usually a result of lava erupting from the same vent, whose weight exceeds the cone's strength.

caldera large, commonly circular, fault-bounded depression on a volcano, caused by collapse due to the removal of magma from a subjacent magma chamber.

clastogenic 'formed from fragments'; often used to describe a lava flow formed by the accumulation on the ground of still-molten or ductile pyroclasts, *cf.* spatter, which builds up around the vent rather than flowing away.

coulée   elongate lava dome; short steep-sided lava extrusion on a dome, often characterised by a wrinkled or blocky surface.

debris avalanche (volcanic)   a gravity-propelled mass flow of volcaniclastic debris, moving in the absence of significant amounts of water (*cf.* lahar), caused by structural failure of a volcanic edifice. Typically deposits consist of large coherent blocks dispersed in a poorly sorted pulverized matrix and may have a hummocky surface.

DRE   Dense Rock Equivalent = the volume of a unit of pumice or other inflated tephra, recalculated to the value it would have if the tephra were 'deflated' (compressed) back to a standard density of 2.7 g cm^{-3}, close to that the magma would have had prior to vesiculation and eruption.

endogenous   describing a lava dome that has grown by swelling due to emplacement of new magma in the interior (*cf.* exogenous).

eruption column the turbulent, ascending part of the ash cloud above an explosive eruption vent.

eutaxitic   describes the texture of a welded tuff in which the pumice clasts and ash shards have been flattened to form fiamme, either during emplacement or by post-emplacement compaction.

evolved   synonym for fractionated.

exogenous   describes a lava dome that has grown by successive accretion of lava erupted from summit vents (*cf.* endogenous)

felsic   describes a rock (eg phonolite, rhyolite) that is rich in light-coloured minerals such as feldspar and quartz, or (if glassy) in the chemical components that make up those minerals (SiO_2, Al_2O_3, Na_2O, K_2O). Also used as collective adjective for such light minerals, *cf.* mafic.

fiamme   strongly flattened pumice clasts characteristic of a welded pyroclastic deposit.

fire fountaining   mildly explosive eruptions in which molten fragments are ejected to relatively low altitude and fall back to the ground in a sufficiently hot condition to form welded spatter deposits and possibly clastogenic (spatter-fed) lava. See Fig. 29. Most common in hawaiian basalt eruptions but a distinctive feature of certain phonolite eruptions in Tenerife, whose proximal products exhibit such features.

fractional crystallisation   partial crystallisation in a magma chamber under conditions (*i.e.* relatively rapid cooling) that isolate later melt fractions from earlier products of crystallisation, inhibiting re-equilibration between them. Such conditions favour the production of more evolved or fractionated residual melts.

fractionated   describes the composition of a magma that has undergone significant fractional crystallization or has evolved chemically in other ways; a fractionated magma is richer in Na, K, volatiles and incompatible elements than the parent magma, and poorer in Mg and Fe.

hawaiian fire-fountaining style of eruption of basaltic magma characterised by fountaining to modest heights such that the magma remains molten on falling to the ground (where it may form a spatter cone or lava lake), *cf.* strombolian.

hawaiite fine-grained intermediate volcanic rock of the alkali basalt-trachyte series (see Fig. 39 right).

ignimbrite a deposit formed from a pumice-rich pyroclastic flow. Some ignimbrites, but by no means all, exhibit welding.

juvenile refers to the newly formed magmatic products of the eruption under consideration (*e.g.* pumice), as opposed to lithic clasts of rock formed in earlier eruptions that were solid at the time of this eruption.

lahar catastrophic slurry of pyroclastic debris and water accelerated by gravity down the slopes and ravines of a volcanic edifice following heavy rain, summit snow-melt, or crater lake outburst. Deposits are characteristically very poorly sorted with a muddy matrix.

lapilli-tuff a pyroclastic rock or deposit formed primarily of pyroclasts of lapilli size (2-64 mm) set in a finer-grained (ash) matrix. Most ignimbrites consist of pumice lapilli-tuff.

lateral collapse subsidence of part of a volcano as a result of a landslide or debris avalanche of an over-steepened flank. See Table 3. Synonym of sector collapse.

lava dome a lava extrusion that is thick in relation to its lateral extent and almost circular in plan view; typical of viscous felsic lavas.

lava tube a conduit in the interior of a pahoehoe lava through which lava continues to flow after the remainder of the flow has solidified; a tunnel-like void from which lava drained and was not replenished.

lithic as used here, a fragment of solid, previously erupted (non-juvenile) or basement rock. Lithic clasts in a pyroclastic deposit may, for example, have been torn from the volcanic vent during an explosive eruption.

mafic describing a rock rich in dark minerals such as olivine, pyroxene and/or amphibole, or (if glassy) in the chemical constituents of those minerals (Mg, Fe). Also used as collective adjective for such dark minerals, *cf.* felsic.

magma a hot silicate liquid in which crystals and/or vesicles may be suspended or dispersed. The term therefore embraces multiphase assemblages comprising melt ± crystals ± gas bubbles, whereas melt refers to material wholly in the molten state.

mantle bedding a characteristic of pyroclastic fall deposits whereby the bed blankets undulating topography with a uniform thickness (at a given distance

Glossary of volcanological terms

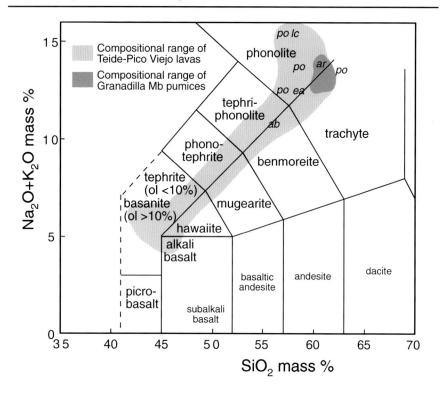

Fig. 39. Current nomenclature for sodic alkaline volcanic rocks: geochemical definitions based on total alkali versus silica plot (after Le Maitre, 2002). A different series of names applies to potassic alkaline rocks (ibid). The mean compositions of selected Bandas del Sur pyroclastic units are shown for reference (after Bryan et al, 2002, using formation names from Brown *et al*, 2003): ea = Abrigo Fm ignimbrite, lc = La Caleta Fm pumice fall, po = various ignimbrites of the Poris Fm, ab = Abades Fm ignimbrite, ar = Arico Fm ignimbrite; the ranges of composition of Teide-Pico Viejo lavas (Ablay *et al* 1998) and Granadilla pumices are shown as grey fields.

from the vent), rather than being concentrated in valleys or depressions. See Box 1.

mugearite   a fine-grained intermediate volcanic rock of the alkali basalt-trachyte series (see Fig. 39 above); more evolved than hawaiite.

nuée ardente   block-and-ash flow that is hot enough for blocks to be incandescent.

obsidian   black or green volcanic glass of evolved composition (typically phonolite in Tenerife).

outflow facies   a distal pyroclastic succession exposed outside a caldera margin,
as distinct from the proximal intra-caldera facies deposited on the caldera
floor. Ignimbrites outside a caldera are typically thinner.

pahoehoe (pron. 'pa-hoey-hoey') Hawaiian word for the form of lava that has a
smooth or regularly wrinkled or ropy upper surface representing deformation of the ductile glassy skin by the drag of lava flowing beneath.
Typically forms from low-viscosity basalt lava flows.

peralkaline   describing the composition of a rock or magma in which the ratio
(Na+K):Al (expressed in atomic, not weight percent, terms) exceeds
1.00.

periclinal   describes a structure dipping outward on all sides from a central apex.

phonolite   silica-undersaturated felsic volcanic rock. A feldspathoid-bearing trachyte. See Fig. 39 above.

phreatic   describes an explosion caused by the explosive conversion of water to
steam through interaction with hot rock. Ejecta consist solely of lithic
(country rock) clasts with no juvenile (magmatic) component.

phreatomagmatic describes an explosion caused by the explosive conversion of
water to steam through interaction with hot magma. Often excavates a
circular crater which may fill with water (maar). Ejecta in the surrounding tuff-ring consist of lithic (country rock) clasts together with juvenile
(magmatic) material, *e.g.* scoria or pumice.

phyric   = porphyritic. Often used to specify the type of phenocryst, thus
'feldspar-phyric' or 'olivine-pyroxene-phyric'.

plinian   style of explosive volcanic eruption characterised by a high (>10 km)
eruptive column (cloud) of pumice and ash, causing the widespread dis-
persal of pumiceous tephra.

pumice   microvesicular volcanic 'foam' formed when the confining pressure on a
volatile-rich felsic magma in a sub-volcanic chamber is released. Typical
of plinian eruptions.

pyroclastic fall deposit   pyroclastic material deposited by gravitational settling
of individual tephra particles through the air. Pyroclastic fall deposits are
characterised by being relatively well sorted (*i.e.* clast-supported) but
often poorly bedded (Box 1). They mantle underlying topography with
an even thickness at any one locality (mantle bedding), though thickness
and clast size decrease with increasing distance from vent.

pyroclastic flow   a rapidly moving density current of hot gas and pyroclastic
debris, dominated either by pumice (producing an ignimbrite) or by
blocks of lithic material and ash (producing a block-and-ash flow).
Pyroclastic flow deposits are poorly sorted with a large proportion of fine
ash (thus clasts are matrix-supported), may be massive or show internal

bedding, and typically thicken into ravines and depressions (Box 1).

pyroclastic fountaining   *cf.* fire fountaining

pyroclastic surge a rapidly moving, turbulent, dilute ash cloud consisting mainly of hot ash and gas. Pyroclastic surge deposits, which commonly show laminar bedding or cross stratification, are now considered to form part of a continuum with pyroclastic flow deposits (except in the case of base surge deposits).

ramping, ramp structure   style of deformation in which rearward (or central) parts of a lava flow or welded tuff ride up over forward (or peripheral) parts, giving a series of arcuate surface ridges.

rheomorphic, -ism   post-depositional flowage of a welded tuff that has remained hot for sufficient time to deform in a ductile manner, resulting in flow-folds, ramp structures and flow breccia.

scoria   dark coloured (usually basaltic) vesiculated lava, usually as clasts.

scoria cone   volcanic cone built of loose clasts of scoria. Typical of a strombolian eruption.

sector collapse   the removal of a major segment of a volcanic edifice by landslide or other gravity-driven process. Sector collapse may be aided by intrusion-related swelling. Synonymous with lateral collapse.

silica-undersaturated   describing the composition of a magma or rock containing too little SiO_2 to crystallise entirely as the silicate minerals pyroxene and feldspar, resulting in the crystallisation of the undersaturated minerals olivine and particularly feldspathoid.

sodalite   a feldspathoid mineral series [$Na_8Al_6Si_6O_{24}(Cl_2,S,SO_4)$] that forms distinctive pale blue phenocrysts in some phonolites and related rocks.

spatter   the deposit formed when still-molten ejecta accumulates near to the base of a lava fountain.

spatter-bank   a positive topographic feature formed by accretion of spatter.

stratovolcano   a layered volcano constructed by alternation of lavas and pyroclastic deposits.

strombolian eruption   style of pyroclastic eruption in which fragments of incandescent, vesiculating mafic magma are fragmented and ejected to a moderate height, landing as solid scoria to form a scoria cone, *cf.* hawaiian.

structural caldera margin   the margin of a caldera, as identified (*e.g.* at a deep erosional level) by the ring fracture within which subsidence has occurred.

surge   see pyroclastic surge.

surtseyan eruption   style of eruption in which ascending basaltic magma interacts explosively with groundwater or surface water. Generates a tuff-ring composed of country rocks clasts with a juvenile component of basaltic clasts and vitric ash, often altered. See phreatomagmatic.

tephriphonolite   see Fig. 39 above.

Glossary of volcanological terms

topographic caldera wall   the margin of a caldera, as identified by an arcuate topographic scarp. As this may have retreated through erosion, a topographic caldera wall generally has a larger radius on a map than the equivalent structural caldera margin.

trachybasalt   loose petrological name originally used to embrace intermediate rock types hawaiite, mugearite and benmoreite (see Fig. 39).

trachyte   fine-grained felsic volcanic rock consisting dominantly of alkali feldpsar; see Fig. 39 above.

transitional   usually denotes a basaltic lava composition transitional between alkali basalt and sub-alkali basalt (see Fig. 39).

turbulent describes motion in a fluid that is irregular and eddying with fluid moving chaotically in all directions, in contrast to laminar flow in which the fluid moves in a uniform direction.

unwelded describes a pyroclastic deposit or rock that has not undergone high-temperature sintering of the glassy ash and pumice fragments.

vertical collapse subsidence of the summit region of a volcano as a result of magma withdrawal from a subjacent magma chamber. See Table 4.

vesicle, vesicular vesicles are gas bubbles preserved in a lava or pyroclast. They signify that the magma became supersaturated with dissolved gas during the course of eruption.

vitrophyre   a pyroclastic deposit so intensely welded as to have become black and glassy.

vulcanian eruption   short-duration pyroclastic explosions forming stratified, poorly sorted ash deposits with a high proportion of lithic blocks and bombs, and only a small juvenile component. Vulcanian eruptions commonly represent a 'throat-clearing' explosion in which solid material blocking a volcanic vent is ejected by the build-up of gas pressure beneath it.

welding, welded compaction and sintering of hot glassy pumice clasts in a pyroclastic flow (or less commonly a fall) deposit. Most commonly recognised in the field by the pronounced welding foliation of hot, ductile pumice clasts to form fiamme (eutaxitic texture - see Box 2)). Welding texture is also exhibited by some obsidian clasts in the Arico ignimbrite (stop 4.4).

ERRATA AND UPDATES (GA GUIDE 49, 2ND EDITION) APRIL 2012

1. The bottom left cell of Table 3 should read 'Main proponents'

2. The location for Stop 4.2 (p. 39) should read '... small quarry west of *Los Blanquitos* school house'. Entrance to quarry is near the Los Blanquitos road sign.

3. Line 4 in the caption to Fig. 18 (p. 55) should read 'Martí et al (1995) *as La Caleta ignimbrite*, but is now believed to be the Abrigo ignimbrite (M. Branney,'.

4. The first paragraph on p. 78 should be deleted. 6. On p. 81, footnote 18 should refer to Fig. 39, not Fig. G1.

5. On p. 86, insert 'lava' after 'clastogenic' in the bottom line. 8. On p.88, the first sentence of the final paragraph should be deleted.

6. On p.92, the caption to Fig. 38 (line 6) refers to a 'pinkish area'. Owing to a slight shift in colour balance during printing, this area now appears light orange.

Corrections to Glossary

The following definitions replace incorrect or misleading definitions in the original glossary:

phreatomagmatic describes the explosive interaction between magma and *groundwater*, forming a tuff ring of juvenile and country-rock ejecta. **surtseyan** describes an explosive eruption arising from violent interaction between ascending magma and *surface* (sea or lake) water.

UPDATES

1. As of Jan 2004, visits to Barranco del Infierno (excursion 1.1) need to be booked in advance (Tel 922 782885) and a charge of €3 per person paid on arrival.

2. Leaders of large parties using coaches should note that the itineraries for Days 2 (Teno by TF436) and 4 (Bandas del Sur via TF28) and stop 5.3 (Mirador de Don Martin on the TF28) are not suitable for coaches with more than 35 seats.

3. The footnote 10 on page 26 should read 'This dyke swarm, like those of the Anaga peninsula, reflects structural controls acting on an individual OBS centre at the time of its construction (Fig. 2), and bears no relation to the structural architecture of the post-OBS edifice (cf. Carracedo and Day, 2002 Fig. 1.3).' A recent paper by Walter and Schmincke (2002) examines the history of rifting and sector collapse during the construction of the Teno OBS volcano [Rifting, recurrent landsliding and Miocene structural reorganization on NW Tenerife (Canary Islands). *International Journal of Earth Sciences* **91**, 615-28].

4. Page 30: the TF-1421 has now been closed owing to persistent rock fall. Turn R directly on to the TF-421 *before* reaching Garachico.

5. Stop 2.8 (pp 30-1). Most of the lava platform on which the town of Garachico is built predates the 1706 eruption (Carmen Solana, University of Portsmouth). The 1706 lavas in Garachico consist of two lobes: (a) one that destroyed the western outskirts of the town and overwhelmed much of the harbour area SW of the church; a small park here highlights how far into the present town the old harbour originally extended.(b) a later lobe now forming the slightly higher ground directly to the east of the convent (a prominent building with two courtyards in the centre of town). Details are given by Solana and Aparicio (1999) in Firth, C.R. and McGuire, W.J. (eds): *Volcanoes in the Quaternary*. Geol. Soc. London Special Publication **161**, 209-216. More westerly components of the 1706 flow field can be seen as fresh a'a flows along the TF-82 road to Santiago around El Tanque (an inland village that was also devastated by the eruption).

6. The Parque Nacional office in Santa Cruz now issues Teide summit permits for a specified 2-hour time slot *on a single day*, not two consecutive days as stated on p 86.

7. The best descent from the rim of Pico Viejo (pp 93-4, Excursion 8.3) is to traverse at a high level round to the western slopes overlooking Las Narices del Teide, where a clear trail descends across steep scree to the upper scoria cone and then down its southern flank to a winding vehicle track that leads in the direction of Boca Tauce.

8. Optional change to Day 5: Rather than take exit 13 to El Escobonal in travelling from stop 5.2 to 5.3 (Mirador de Don Martin), it is worth exiting at junction 14 and driving up to Fasnia (TF620). This road winds round a prominent flank scoria cone that has been blankleted by a plinian pumice fall deposit, and the related ignimbrite can be seen beside the road NW of the cone. The relationships provide evidence that basaltic flank eruptions continued during the late Cañadas phase of large-scale pyroclastic eruptions

9. Stop 9.2. Montaña de la Horca is disfigured by a large hotel complex. The best overview of the sub-historic cones in the Orotava valley is obtained from the mirador/café overlooking Tigaiga on the road from Los Realejos to Icod el Alto; roadcuts also expose pyroclastics and debris avalanche deposits in the western wall of the landslide-carved valley.

10. The volcanology text by the late Peter Frances is available in a new 2003 edition (co-authored by Clive Oppenheimer, OUP ISBN 0-19-925469-9).

11. The caldera geology summarized in Figs. 23 and 28 is rewarding to view in Google Earth (http://earth.google.co.uk/).

12. In April 2009, Linda Fowler of the Open University reported a change to Stop 4.2; she says ' the essential part of the La Cantera schoolhouse exposure is not going to be accessible in future as there is building going on which is covering the whole of the quarry floor area and will shortly obscure the face'. In future she'll be using the El Desierto cutting (down the road to San Isidro) in future; this has reasonable parking at the top end and is a fair substitute, showing erosion of the fall deposit by the flow, and some cemented ash horizons in the fall.

NEW LOCALITIES Stop 9.4 Hotel Maritímo debris avalanche deposit (courtesy of Dr Juan-Carlos Carracedo)

An outcrop of the debris avalanche deposit flooring the Orotava landslide valley can be seen in sea cliffs SW of the Hotel Maritímo, a complex of prominent blue tower blocks not far from the eastern end of the TF5 motorway west of Puerto de la Cruz. Take the exit for Punta Brava, cross the main road (TF42) and continue down through the town of Longuera (one-way system), forking left on leaving the town where signed to Hotel Maritímo, and turning left into the carpark in front of the Hotel Maritímo near to the coast (a relief carpark suitable for coaches is available on the right of the road shortly before reaching the hotel). Walk to western end of the main carpark and descend to the tourist footpath that traverses about half way up the cliffs ahead. Massive polylithic clast-supported debris avalanche breccia is exposed in the cliff. The deposit has steep, though poorly exposed, contacts against lavas on both sides (also forms 3 sea stacks); from the headland to the NW, a path descends to the beach where these relationships can be examined.

Stop 9.5 Tuff-ring deposits surrounding the Caldera del Rey phreatomagmatic tuff ring near Playa de las Americas.

Turn off the TF1 Autopista del Sur (heading NW) at Junction 30. Filter right off the service road immediately on passing under a bridge. Take the second turn on the right ('Calle Madrid'). Tuff-ring deposits are exposed on both sides of the lower stretch of this road, showing marked cross-bedding in alternating beds of coarse lapilli and finer ash typical of tuff ring deposits (see Cas and Wright, 1987, p. 378). Bomb sags (cf. ibid Fig. 13.20) and related bedding contortion beneath ballistic ejecta, indicating trajectories emanating from the vicinity of the Caldera del Rey crater, may be seen in several places on the right-hand side. Indistinct chute and pool structures can also be seen in places, suggesting **base surge** deposition.

For an overview of the Caldera del Rey structure, return to the bottom of Calle Madrid and turn right. The road winds its way uphill past endless recent holiday developments (keep right at a monstrous arch). Take a left turn to follow the road to its very highest point, which offers a view over the crater/tuff cone. The floor of the elongated cone has been exploited for intensive agriculture.

Stop 9.6 Sole mark casts at the base of the Abrigo ignimbrite near Puerto de Santiago.

Sole marks, which are common in turbidites, have been observed as casts where a small cavern has been eroded out under the Abrigo Ignimbrite just south of Puerto de Santiago. They were engraved by pebble to cobble-sized lithic tools in a soft, cohesive fine-grained substrate. The casts range from long, parallel groove marks, often with the tool embedded at their termination, to short, elongate impact marks and are useful as a flow-direction marker. Pittari and Cas (see the reference below) argue that they were formed from a highly energetic pyroclastic flow pulse, and were almost immediately infilled with ash after rapid waning of flow. Large lithic tools, which formed groove marks, were held in place under high gas and grain dynamic pressures and moved forward by their own momentum and the drag force exerted by a highly concentrated granular flow. The implications of these sole marks for ignimbrite transport and deposition mechanisms (Guide, Box 2) can be discussed.

Adrian Pittari provides the following directions (kindly passed on to me by Linda Fowler at the Open University): drive west and then north on the main road up the west coast, but after Adeje, turn left onto TF47 towards the coast. Stay on the coast road, past Callao Salvaje, Playa San Juan and Alcalá. About 2km past Alcalá and 500m before the turn off to Puerto de Santiago, on the left is open farmland facing out to sea. When we were there in 2004 there was a lot of construction site debris (large rock boulders) on the farmland between the road and the coast. Turn left onto a dirt road at the northern end of this open area just before a group of houses (El Varadero). The dirt road turns southwards and follows a cobble beach (Callao Chico). There are likely to be people camping along this road above the beach. The exposure of the Abrigo Ignimbrite forms a small headland at the southern end of this cobble beach (Punta Blanca). There is plenty of parking on top of the exposure or on the side of the road nearby. Be careful walking down to the exposure and onto the ledge – it is steep but only a couple of metres down, and the ledge is narrow. There is only room for about 5-10 people at a time. This location is easiest at low tide. For a detailed description and interpretation of the sole marks, see the original article by Adrian Pittari and Ray Cas

(Sole marks at the base of the late Pleistocene Abrigo Ignimbrite, Tenerife: implications for transport and depositional processes at the base of pyroclastic flows. *Bulletin of Volcanology* **66/4** 356-63, 2004).

A short walk around the 'Volcán Garachico' (= Montaña Negra) from the Arenas Negras car park (TF-38) features in the Rother walking guide to Tenerife (K. Wolfsperger and A. Wolfsperger, 2001, *Tenerife- The finest valley and mountain walks*, Rother ISBN 3763348093 – recommended by Alan Peacegood).

Readers interested in the hydrogeological and water supply problems on Tenerife should visit www.aguastenerife.org (in Spanish - . Further corrections, updates and suggestions will be welcomed. Please e-mail robingill@f2s.com.

Other Guides published by the Geologists' Association:

Rockwatch Guide No. 1 'A Pocket Guide to the London Clay exposed on the North Shore of the Isle of Sheppey, Kent'

Additional guides and current prices are available from:
The Executive Secretary, Geologists' Association,
Burlington House, Piccadilly, London W1J 0DU
Telephone: 020 7434 9298
E-mail: admin@geologistsassociation.org.uk
Website: www.geologistsassociation.org.uk